THE ATHLETIC SKIER

THE ATHLETIC SKIER

Warren Witherell
and
David Evrard

Drawings by David Evrard & Diane Bode

Photos by Erik Ostling & Thor Kallerud

Book Design by Mike Reynolds

Published by The Athletic Skier Inc.

Cover Design by Rob Magiera
Cover Photo by Randy Klamm / Skier: Torjus Berge

Additional drawings by Viki Fleckenstein Woodworth and Julie Lewis

Additional photographs by Team Russell, Hiro Yakushi, Zoom, Pentaphoto, Tom DeCarlo, Byron Hetzler, David Brownell, Tom King, Scott Markowitz, John Claussen, and Debra Dietz.

Third Printing - 1998
9 8 7 6 5 4 3

Library of Congress Cataloging-in-Publication Data
Witherell, Warren.
The Athletic Skier / Warren Witherell & David Evrard : drawings by David Evrard : photos by Erik Ostling & Thor Kallerud.
     p.   cm.
  ISBN 1-55566-117-3 : $24.95
  1. Skis and skiing. 2. Skis and skiing—Training. 3. Ski racing.
I. Evrard, David. II. Title.
GV854.W53   1993
796.93—dc20   93-30516
                                  CIP

THE ATHLETIC SKIER is published by
The Athletic Skier Inc.
P.O. Box 21315
Salt Lake City, Utah 84121-21315

Printed by Johnson Printing
A Division of Johnson Publishing Company
1880 South 57th Court
Boulder, Colorado 80301
(303) 443-1576

Distributed by Johnson Books
A Division of Johnson Publishing Company
1880 South 57th Court
Boulder, Colorado 80301
(800) 258-5830

To our parents —

who gave us many opportunities to become athletes.

Table of Contents

Meet the Authors

Warren Witherell and David Evrard met at Alta, Utah, in 1988. In the years since, they have spent many days skiing together. Their discussions about ski technique, and their enthusiasm for teaching others to more fully enjoy the sport, have given life to this book.

Warren Witherell has had an enormous influence on American skiing. He began coaching in 1960 in Lake Placid, New York. In 1970, at Burke Mountain, Vermont, he founded the first ski academy in the United States. He served as Headmaster, teacher, and coach at Burke Mountain Academy until 1984. The school has gained national and international recognition not only as a sports training center, but for its achievements in academics and in the development of a values-oriented community.

ERIK OSTLING

Warren's 1972 book, *How the Racers Ski*, was the first book to describe the carved turn and to promote a way of skiing that focused on "balance, economy of motion, and the use of the ski to create turning forces." This approach to skiing fostered a revolutionary change from the Austrian and French techniques then being taught in ski schools around the world. *How the Racers Ski* had a large influence on ski teaching and race coaching not only in the United States but in Europe as well.

Warren began canting boots for ski racers in 1968, and was the first coach to systematically evaluate the canting and fore/aft balance needs of all racers in his program. He has been thinking about "skier alignment" for 25 years. His focus on this subject, in the book you are holding, draws on all these years observing skiers.

In addition to his success as an educator and coach, Warren has had an extraordinary career as an athlete. He has studied sports by doing them. He was an All-American swimmer in high school; won college letters in soccer, hockey, and baseball; has played professional golf; and is enshrined in the Water Ski Hall of Fame. He won his first World Championship in water skiing in 1953, at age 18; and his last at the World Masters Games in 1989, at age 54. He has held numerous U.S. National records in the years between. Warren began racing on snow skis at age 22 and won the Eastern Downhill Championships when he was 27. He has spent most of his life "thinking about how to do things more efficiently in sports."

Warren's coaching career began at age 18—with water skiers. He has since coached soccer, hockey, baseball, and snow skiing. He has been a student of gymnastics, diving, figure skating, and many other sports that involve movement and balance. He says he has been fascinated by how bodies move since he first learned to crawl.

ERIK OSTLING

David Evrard has dedicated his life to the sport of skiing. He is widely respected for his clear and innovative thinking on technical issues, and for his ability to turn concepts into reality.

David has extensive, multinational experience in the ski industry. As a technical consultant, he has created innovations in ski boot design, ski orthotics, and supercooling systems for snowmaking. He has been involved in retail ski shops in both the U.S. and Australia for fifteen years.

David began ski racing at the age of 14 and raced on the Pro Tour from 1977 to 1985. Like most racers of his generation, he was deeply influenced by *How the Racers Ski*. This book provided the foundation for his technical development. His work in skiing has been a logical evolution and clarification of the concepts first described in that book.

David earned his PSIA instructor certification in 1976, and has long been an advocate of student-centered instruction. His knowledge of ski teaching, physiology, biomechanics, and sport training are reflected in all parts of this book.

Foreword

by Thor Kallerud
Men's Head Technical Coach
United States Ski Team

DEBRA DIETZ

When Warren Witherell published *How the Racers Ski* in the early seventies, he defined a revolutionary concept for alpine skiers. Instead of using the skis primarily to skid and slide in the turn, Warren advocated the carving of precise turns. His idea was to take more advantage of the design of skis, enabling skiers to produce clean "narrow tracks" on the mountain sides.

Just prior to the publication of *How the Racers Ski,* a technological breakthrough took place which produced a more supportive ski boot. At the same time, new ski designs with different geometry and construction materials were introduced. The concept of skiing that Warren developed took advantage of these features.

Now, two decades later, skiing is witnessing another technological breakthrough with newer ski geometry and even better construction materials. In the ever evolving world of alpine skiing, technological advancements are offering exciting opportunities for skiers at all levels to improve their carving skills. Recreational skiers have equipment that is as precise and functional for their carving needs as the best race skis are for World Cup racers. In this book, Warren Witherell and David Evrard define what the best skiers are doing, and what is possible for all skiers to learn.

The top athletes on the World Cup circuit are now able to ski more cleanly carved turns, and to carve turns of a smaller radius. They are making balanced turns with their center of mass travelling a shorter path than their skis. The best racers emphasize the blending of impeccable balance and the use of gravity to ski smoothly and efficiently at high speed. We are watching the world's greatest alpine athletes execute beautiful, clean carved turns—just as Warren envisioned it twenty years ago.

During the last decade, few books have been published that deal with modern alpine ski technique and ski technology. Bearing in mind that we have undergone many technical and technological changes, *The Athletic Skier* carves its place in the history of skiing literature. By teaching the movements of the world's best athletes to skiers at all ability levels, this book invites the reader into the enchanting world of alpine skiing in the nineties. It blends the technical and technological features in a unique way with emphasis on balance as the underlying factor for all movement on skis. It also offers unequaled insight into a scientific approach to understand how different adjustments of alpine equipment can influence a skier's performance.

This book offers ideas and concepts that provide both immediate and long term improvements for all skiers. Anyone who is interested in modern ski technique should be challenged and fascinated by *The Athletic Skier*.

September 12, 1993
Park City, Utah

Preface

This book is for all skiers who would like to be better skiers. Whether you are learning wedge turns, or racing on the World Cup, the information you hold in your hands can lift your skiing to a higher level. We have written for weekenders and racers and everyone in between. Though they apply them to different tasks, all skiers depend on the same fundamentals.

We have chosen "the Athletic Skier" for our title because it defines the skier we most admire, and the one we hope many readers will become. Athletes are energetic, find joy in sport, and take every advantage to improve. They are serious about equipment. They take time for training. They set high goals and work to achieve them.

We have tried, in 240 pages, to condense what we've learned in sixty years of racing, teaching, coaching, bootfitting, and having fun every day we skied. In preparing this book, we spent a fascinating year exploring all aspects of skiing with old friends and new. Their contributions to our text have been enormous. We thank them for their knowledge, and pass it on.

Special sections of this book are addressed to ski instructors, racers, and coaches. These chapters are relevant for *all* readers. All students of skiing are a step ahead if they know what instructors know, and understand how they teach. Racers can never know enough about balance and fundamentals. Today's racing skills will be tomorrow's standard for recreational skiing.

This is not a book to be read once and put on a shelf. Many chapters require slow, thoughtful reading. Just as good coaches study their athletes over and over again, you should be rewarded by returning often to study this book. When you finish the whole, if you then return to earlier parts, they will have more meaning.

We'd like to express our appreciation to the photographers and skiers whose images support this text. Many of the skiers have won Olympic and World Championship medals. We're inspired by their athleticism and the efficiency of their technique.

If our readers learn to ski more athletically, and more efficiently, we will have succeeded with this book.

"Ski Fast and Leave Narrow Tracks"

Warren Witherell and David Evrard,
Alta, Utah, 1993.

PART 1

THE ATHLETIC SKIER

"If you apply the correct edge angle and pressure to a ski, and just stand on it, it will take you where you want to go."

"Skiers who dance on a mountain at 30 miles per hour have more fun than those who slip and slide at speeds below fifteen."

Chapter 1

A Philosophy of Skiing and of Teaching Skiing

We love to ski. We are serious athletes. We believe that skiers who dance on a mountain at thirty miles per hour have more fun than those who slip and slide at speeds below fifteen.

When we ski, we like to challenge ourselves and to play with the mountain. We use our skis as accelerators more than brakes. Skiing is sport. It's active, energetic, dynamic. It offers constant challenges to improve.

From chairlifts, we have watched a million skiers—studying their body mechanics and technique. We see clearly what their bodies are doing, but wonder what's in their minds. Most are performing at levels *far below their potential*. They are trying to improve, but lack the knowledge to do so.

If you're one of these athletes—trying to learn, and needing help—we'd like to be your teachers.

Before investing the time to read, it's fair to ask: "What will you teach me? What kind of skiing will I learn here?"

Athletic skiing! We come from racing backgrounds. Speed with precision is our goal, and science is our method. We seek every advantage from equipment. Before we go on snow, we'll adjust your boots and align your body so you can ski in *perfect balance*.

Then we'll teach you to ski—with freedom and flair and a playful spirit. We teach carving skills and economy of motion. We'll help you discover ways of skiing that work best for *your* body, *your* strength, *your* coordination. No two bodies are the same; and no two skiers should ski alike. We'll give you exploring tools, and help you find your talents. We'll teach you to ski a little faster, and with greater safety, too.

Whether you're sixteen or sixty, male or female, beginner or expert—when you ski with us, you're sure to have fun. You don't have to be a super athlete. Just bring whatever ability you have, and let us teach you to exploit it. All you need is a commitment to learn, and an image of the Athletic Skier you can become.

Chapter 2

What Is an Athletic Skier?

If you are watching skiers from a chairlift, and one goes past who inspires the exclamation: "Wow! I'd give *anything* to ski like that"—the chances are good you've seen an athletic skier. What movements, what qualities of skiing have caught your eye?

ATHLETIC SKIERS EXHIBIT THE FOLLOWING TRAITS:

1. Exceptional Balance
2. Dynamic Motion
3. Carving Skills
4. Lateral Movement
5. Strength
6. Quickness and Agility
7. Economy of Motion
8. Relaxation
9. A Natural and Unaffected Style
10. Playfulness and Imagination

The rest of this book will focus on teaching and learning these elements of good skiing. Let's begin with an overview—a brief description of the goals we're working toward.

1. EXCEPTIONAL BALANCE

You must strive for ***perfect balance.*** "Good" balance is never good enough. Accept no compromise. Perfect balance makes optimum performance possible. Imperfect balance inhibits performance.

This book will focus again and again on balance. The word appears like a litany throughout the text. Please share our commitment to addressing balance factors in all aspects of ski technique. ***No other issue is more important to your progress as a skier.***

Optimum balance can only be achieved with boots that work correctly—that provide the right fit, fore/aft balance, flex characteristics, and lateral alignment. We'll address these issues in the next few chapters, and will expand on them often in other parts of the book.

Optimum balance contributes to quickness, agility, relaxation, strength, economy of motion, and carving ability—to virtually all the elements of athletic skiing. (See photo 1.)

Canadian skier, Karen Percy, won Bronze Medals in the Downhill and Super G at the 1988 Calgary Olympics. Note her position with knees forward, hips centered over her boots, and torso erect. The large muscles in her lower back and abdomen are most relaxed in this stance.

We urge you to look carefully at the twelve photos in this chapter. Viewed singly, each photo highlights a particular skill. Taken as a group, they leave a strong impression of *really good* skiing. Absorb these images into your consciousness. Carry them with you as you read, and return to them often. When you get to the mountain, let these images be reflected in your skiing.

2. DYNAMIC MOTION

Reflex mechanisms in the human body work most effectively when in continuous motion. It's more difficult to initiate skiing movements from static positions than from active ones. Ski instructors, when demonstrating one position throughout a turn, are often static. So are the students who copy them. Racers, when skiing from "arc to arc," are more dynamic. Their movements are continuous, integrated and active. They never stop in one position.

A full range of motion—extension and contraction, weighting and unweighting—provides relaxation at the top of the motion and an expanded range of edge control at the bottom. In powder and crud skiing, a full range of motion is particularly important. Lateral movement and flexibility are necessary to ski with good edging skills and strong angulation. (See photo 2.)

ZOOM

Stephanie Schuster (AUT) shows that skiing can be as dynamic and instinctive as running. Her movements here are similar to those of a tailback when turning the corner on an end sweep.

3. CARVING SKILLS

The carved turn provides a foundation for athletic skiing. If you apply correct edge angle and pressure to a ski, the ski itself provides the turning forces you desire. In a pure carved turn, there is no side-slip or skidding. The entire ski edge runs in the same groove, and the ski leaves a track in the snow as in photo 3. Athletic skiers have the ability to put a ski on edge, apply pressure to it, and know it will take them where they want to go.

THOR KALLERUD

Tim Hanson (USA) makes a clean, carved turn. Can you imagine the feelings such turns provide? The stability, precision, and fluid motion are a constant delight to good skiers. Notice the carved turn tracks in the background where racers have been free skiing.

Athletic skiers do not carve all turns. They combine carving and steering as terrain and line demand. While a variety of skills are important to the athletic skier, the carved turn provides the stability and precision that is evident in all good skiing. Racers ski "from arc to arc" whenever possible. ***The mastery of carving skills should be the goal of all recreational skiers as well.*** (See photo 4.)

TEAM RUSSELL

Urs Lehmann (SUI) carves on a clean edge. Notice how little snow is displaced by the ski. Lehmann won the DH at the 1993 World Championships.

4. LATERAL MOVEMENT

The single most distinguishing trait of athletic skiers is the ability to ski in balance when their feet are far to one side of their bodies. Photo 5 shows Diann Roffe Steinrotter in perfect balance on her outside ski though she has more than 70 degrees of inclination. Her right ski is edged nearly 80 degrees. Can you see yourself in this position? This requires the skill and equipment of a world class skier. In the next turn Diann makes, her feet may be as far to her left as they are to her right in this turn. Diann's turn shows an extreme range of lateral movement.

5

PENTAPHOTO

Diann Roffe Steinrotter (USA) displays the skills that won her a Silver Medal in GS at the 1992 Olympics, and the Gold in Super G at the 1994 Olympics.

Photo 6 shows a 58-year-old man free skiing at Deer Valley. His inclination is 40 degrees, and his feet are a long way from under his body. He's cruising, and is very relaxed. Diann is working harder, but is equally relaxed. Both skiers are in their comfort zones.

Athletic skiers display a wide divergence of lines between their center of mass (CM) and their feet. The CM is stable, while the feet move dynamically under it. Excellent carving skills are required to support the angulation Diann and Warren exhibit. If their skis slip, they will fall. But their skis do not slip. Their edges hold, and they are stable on a carving ski. From this platform, athletic skiers can move through a wide range of motion with relative ease. When you have the right skills, skiing is easier than running!

6

ERIK OSTLING

Warren Witherell's skiing shows a broad range of lateral movement supported by carving skills.

If you think of running a dry land slalom course in soccer shoes, you will have an image of strong lateral movement. For each turn, your feet must move laterally more than your center of mass. If you wear cleats, your range of lateral movement is greater than in tennis shoes. For skiers, ***carving skills are like cleats:*** they extend their range of lateral motion. The best skiers exhibit the greatest range of motion—and have the most fun.

5. STRENGTH

A surplus of strength rewards skiers with tremendous freedom. Insufficient strength is always limiting. Those who are strongest can do easily what others can't attempt. The strong can jump from higher cliffs and power their way through crud or heavy snow. They hold carved turns on tighter arcs and at higher speeds. When stresses are high, those with a reserve of strength can sustain graceful and relaxed movement. Strength is essential to racing, and defines the limits of carving in all free skiing. *(See photo 7.)*

HIRO YAKUSHI

Mathias Berthold (AUT) maintains perfect control of his skis though he is clearly in a difficult position. Notice how well his right ski is carving and holding in the snow. This helps him to remain agile and well balanced. A surplus of strength allows Berthold to perform with ease and precision in a situation that would overwhelm most skiers. Mathias' movement is active and dynamic. He exhibits grace under pressure. Strength makes this possible.

6. QUICKNESS AND AGILITY

Quickness and agility are enhanced by optimum balance and inhibited by poor balance. It is difficult to make quick moves from a skidding ski. (A skid is inherently unstable in all athletic movement.) A solid platform, provided by a carving ski, is necessary for quick movement. An athletic stance, with the knees bent and the upper body erect, contributes to agility. It helps, also, to have your eyes focused well ahead of your skis. Relaxation, both mental and physical, also contributes to quickness and agility. Relaxation is enhanced by good balance. (See photo 8.)

Michelle McKendry (CAN) shows agility at 60 MPH. It is clear she departed the snow from the solid platform of a carving ski; and she is confident the same ski edge will support her when she lands.

7. ECONOMY OF MOTION

Economy of motion is fundamental to success in sports. The laws of physics tell us that every action has an equal and opposite reaction. Thus, all extraneous movements are compounded by their balancing movements. *Muscles that are busy doing one task are less efficient at doing others.* As unnecessary movements are reduced, muscles can work with greater efficiency. (See photo 9.)

9

ZOOM

Carole Merle (FRA) shows the efficiency common to the best skiers. She is perfectly balanced; hand and arm motions are well disciplined; she lets her skis create turning forces. While skiing dynamically, she gets a maximum response from minimum effort. Carole won the GS at the 1993 World Championships.

8. RELAXATION

We ski for fun. Relaxation is critical to fluid movement, to rhythm, to quickness, and to a sense of freedom. It's important to choose terrain on which you can ski well. Technical skills are best learned on slopes that encourage aggressive, confident skiing. On difficult terrain, you ski with too much tension—reinforcing static and defensive habits. It's good for the ego to conquer the steeps; but it's good for technique to ski loose and relaxed. Sometimes, the most fun you can have is on easy terrain. When carving skills are used, surprisingly high speeds can result, while relaxation is maintained. Skidding creates tension. A flowing, carving ski provides a stable platform and enhances relaxation.

An upright stance, or what coaches call "a proud position," contributes significantly to relaxation—allowing muscles to rest and bones to carry weight. Photo 10 is of Scot Schmidt, one of the leading extreme skiers in the world. In numerous photos throughout this book, he exhibits a delightful relaxation in his skiing.

TEAM RUSSELL

10

9. A NATURAL AND UNAFFECTED STYLE

Ski technique should be natural, comfortable, and spontaneous. Functional skiing should prevail over "pretty" skiing. There is no "correct form" or "proper position" that all should copy. People who teach skiing, whether instructors, coaches, or friends, too often demonstrate "correct positions" which become static when forced on others. Spontaneity and dynamic motion, as shown by Karen Percy in photo 11, should be stressed at all levels of ski instruction. Skiing should be as natural and unselfconscious as walking or running.

TEAM RUSSELL

11

Karen Percy displays unusual spontaneity in her skiing. She is never "posed". Her movements are as natural and unselfconscious as those of a child when playing hopscotch, or a good athlete jumping from one boulder to another when running in a stream bed. Ski school purists may complain that Karen's left hand is in an "uncorrect" position. We think the movement of her left arm demonstrates a natural athleticism that is entirely appropriate for the specific "turn" or movement Karen is making. There is no name for this turn. It is one unique movement among millions she will create in a season. Karen skis with a sense of freedom all skiers should develop. In this single photo, we can see all the qualities of an athletic skier: Good balance, dynamic motion, carving skills, lateral movement, strength, agility, economy of motion, relaxation, and playfulness. This is the kind of skiing we teach in this book.

10. PLAYFULNESS AND IMAGINATION

Skiing is play. We learn and perform best when we're having fun, exploring and experimenting. Learn to play with your skis—to dance on your edges, to feel the snow, to create turns in a variety of subtle and imaginative ways. Sing when you ski. Dance to different rhythms. Be delicate one moment and powerful the next. Be forever curious about the variety of responses you can generate between your skis and the snow. Ski fast, catch air, and laugh often. (See photo 12.)

Summation: Our goal throughout this book is to help skiers develop the skills required for athletic skiing. We approach this task quite differently from most ski schools or other "instruction" books. We take the broader perspective of a coach—looking at all issues that affect performance: equipment, training, knowledge, technique, and goal setting. *Our goals are high for all skiers.* We know that most people can learn to ski *much better than they imagine.*

This book is for skiers who are serious about learning. Progress in athletics is seldom easy, but always rewarding. If you enjoy learning as much as we enjoy teaching, we'll make a good team.

*Facing page: Pam Fletcher, former
USST downhiller, still enjoys air time.*

"Only when properly canted can our bodies and skis work as efficiently as possible. . . . Nearly all skiers should be canted so their knees are between 1 and 2.5 degrees inside of vertical when their skis are flat".

PART 2

BOOTS AND BALANCE: THE SUSPENSION SYSTEM

The quality of skiing demonstrated in the photos you have just seen can only be achieved by athletes who are *perfectly* balanced. Good balance for skiers is determined not only by their athletic ability, but also by their boots. *You cannot become a versatile and athletic skier until your boot, body, and suspension systems are perfectly aligned.*

Ideally, boots position skiers in good balance and support their needs for athletic movement. In fact, **most skier's boots position them out of balance, and make athletic skiing difficult.**

Ninety percent of all the skiers we observe are handicapped by their boots. Some have small handicaps, some large. In our view, all handicaps that limit one's joy or achievement in skiing are unacceptable!

On many levels, this book is a battle against complacency. We are not happy to mush along in ignorance—skidding our skis, slopping around in our boots, or compensating for alignment problems. We know the joys of skiing in perfect balance, and we want to share them with you.

Only when you get your suspension system right, can you become the *best skier* your natural talents permit. Getting it right is a daunting task. It will take 50 pages of this book to show you how; and a determined effort on your part to apply what you learn. The rewards will be worth your effort.

If skiers come to us for lessons on snow, the first thing we do is check their alignment, see how their boots work, and adjust them as necessary. Only when boot functions and alignment are right, do we go skiing. We must teach the same way in this book. "Why," you may ask, "are boots so important?"

A ski boot is an exoskeleton in which we place our foot and lower leg. When tightly closed, the boot becomes an extension of our leg. It is both an ally and an enemy in the tasks of skiing. We need the boot's strength to apply forces to our skis; but its rigid structure determines our alignment—for better or worse. Rigid boots restrict the freedom of movement and natural balance a more flexible foot allows. To ski well, a perfect combination of support, alignment, and flexibility must be found.

What must a boot do? First, with the greatest possible efficiency, it must transmit forces to our skis. These forces are sometimes powerful and other times subtle. Second, a boot must support our bodies *in the best possible balance* through the entire range of motion that skiing demands. These are large assignments.

No boot manufacturer can do more than make a boot that fits a norm. Like fingerprints, feet and legs are all different. Skiers, therefore, must customize their boots so they *fit* perfectly and *function* perfectly. The fit is the easy part, and bootfitters in many ski shops provide good service.

To make boots "function" or "work" as well as possible is a more complex task, and one few bootfitters are trained for. For this task we need not just a boot*fitter*, but an *alignment specialist*. This person needs a pedorthist's knowledge of feet, a coach's knowledge of technique, a host of mechanical skills, and supporting equipment from the ski industry. ***Everyone in skiing needs to better understand how boot function affects skier performance.***

When bootfitters, skiers, instructors, and manufacturers share the same knowledge and goals—then we can get the suspension system right for every skier.

The next four chapters are addressed to the bootfitter and the boot user who must work together as a team.

Chapter 3

SKIER ASSESSMENT

W e think of a skier's legs, feet, boots, and bindings as an integrated *"suspension system."* When this *entire system* is perfectly aligned, athletic skiing is enhanced. If any part of the system is mis-aligned, performance is diminished. Balance, efficiency, power, and quickness are supported by good alignment.

Skier alignment is not an exact science. There are so many different foot shapes, leg shapes, and body builds that every skier must be seen as an individual with special needs. These complexities, however, should not deter us from sensible action. The guidelines that follow are helpful for all skiers.

To determine a skier's alignment needs, we start with an overview: ***Our objective is to support and align the skier in the most balanced and efficient position possible.***

There are five adjustable components in the alignment system: One is the skier's body; three are in the boot; and the final adjustment is at the boot/ski interface.

All components of this system are interrelated. Adjusting one affects all others. We think of these steps as a circle. It's important to perform the assessment process twice. Precede and follow all adjustments with measurements that confirm and document your intent. You must know where you are before choosing where to go. (See drawing 1, next page.)

Let's review each step in this circle:

1. **Do a skier assessment.** This determines a skier's overall alignment needs.

2. **Build a footbed or orthotic.** This supports or corrects the foot as needed.

3. **Provide fore/aft balance.** This is done by adjusting forward lean, flex, and heel height inside or outside the boot.

4. **Adjust the boot cuff.** This conforms the boot shaft to the curve of the leg.

5. **Cant as necessary.** This aligns the knee in the most efficient position for skiing.

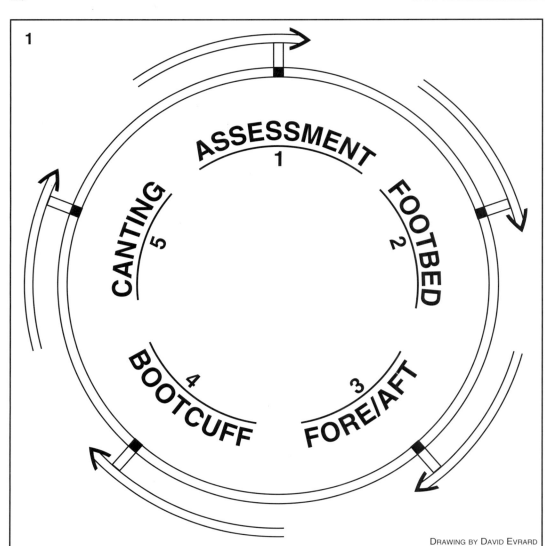

ALIGNMENT CIRCLE

SKIER ASSESSMENT

To the degree appropriate, assess the skier's physical structure. Identify unusual needs, injuries that require attention, overall strength and fitness. Determine the skier's ability level and goals in skiing.

To proceed the skier must be barefoot and wearing shorts that allow easy examination of the legs. With a pen, draw a vertical line *at the center of knee mass* on each knee. This line will be *on* the kneecap, *but may not be at its center*. This procedure must be done facing each knee squarely. A discriminating eye and good judgement are required here. **Be precise.** (See photo 13.)

13

Erik Ostling

It's extremely important that you identify the exact center of the knee mass. The skier's boots must be parallel, and his/her stance must be perfectly square. To have a clear perspective, you must sit directly in front of the knee as the camera does for this photo.

Next look at the lower legs. How much curve do they have? If they are very curved or extremely straight, make a note for consideration in adjusting the cuff.

The feet are next in the assessment, and are very complicated. Our goals are to support the foot in a neutral alignment and to determine the heel height needed. We must look at the skiers foot in both a weighted, skier's stance and in an unweighted, relaxed state.

In the weighted stance, we are looking for pronation or supination. (See drawings 2 and 3.)

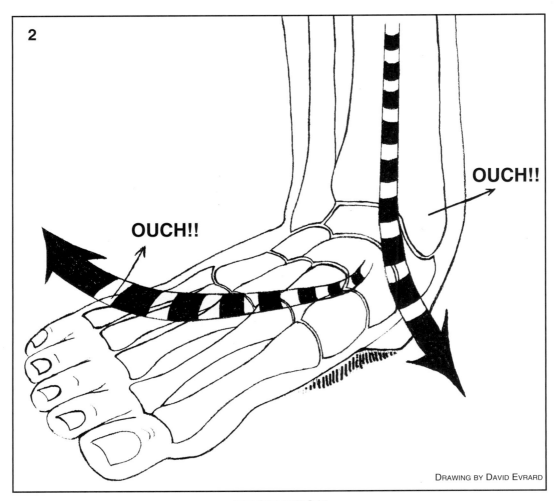

DRAWING BY DAVID EVRARD

PRONATION

The arrows show how forces applied to the foot are misdirected. The ankle rolls inward. The forefoot elongates and splays outward. Instability of the foot, combined with changes in foot shape, cause numerous fit problems in a ski boot. In fact, the sizing and fit of the boot might be fine—IF the foot were properly supported.

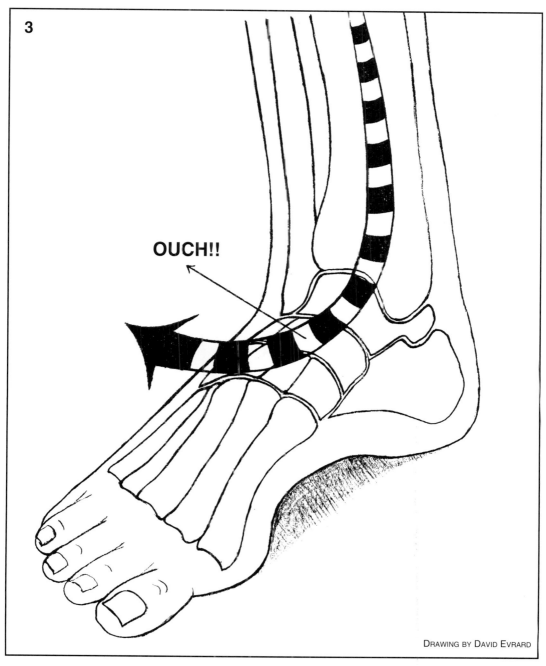

3

OUCH!!

SUPINATION

A supinated foot rolls to the outside when weighted. This creates pressure on the outside ankle bone. Most supinated feet have a high arch. As the foot rolls outward, the arch grows taller. This compresses the top of the foot against the instep of the boot. When the boots are firmly buckled, this compression causes discomfort, a loss of circulation, and impairment of nerve functions.

In the unweighted stance, we observe the sole profile from the outside of the foot. We look at heel level in relation to forefoot level. The amount of difference is the amount of heel lift we want in the footbed. This significantly affects fore/aft balance. (See drawing 4, and see footnotes on page 28 and page 41.)

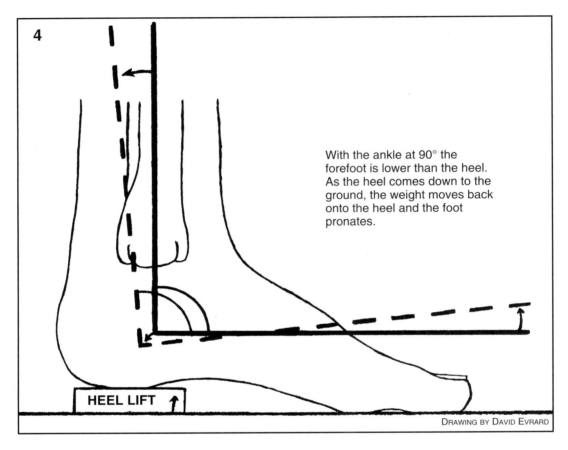

4

With the ankle at 90° the forefoot is lower than the heel. As the heel comes down to the ground, the weight moves back onto the heel and the foot pronates.

HEEL LIFT

Drawing by David Evrard

Some feet are balanced and aligned when the heel and forefoot rest on the same plane. Other feet are best balanced and aligned when the heel is higher than the forefoot. (Note that the heel is raised in most street shoes, athletic trainers, etc.)

The foot drawn here is balanced and aligned with the heel lift as shown (heavy line). If the heel is lowered (dotted line), the weight moves back onto the heel, the foot pronates, and the skier's balance shifts to the rear.

Now it's time to put your boots on and do a preliminary assessment of canting needs. We do this by hanging a plumb-bob from the line on the knee to the front of the bootsole. (See photo 14.)

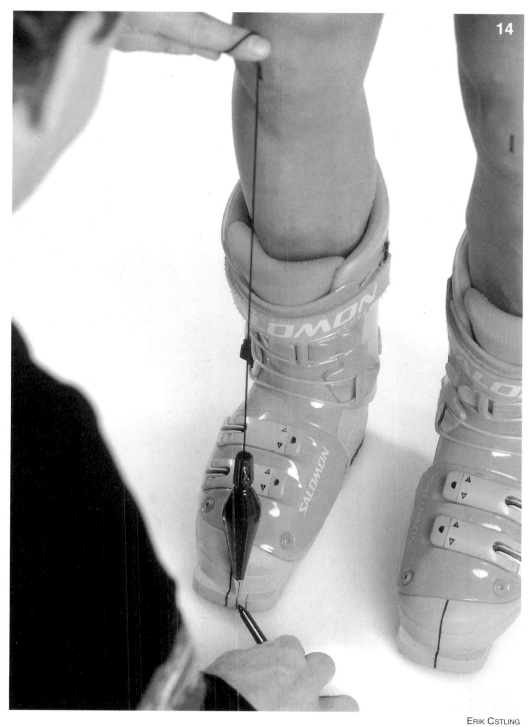

ERIK CSTLING

The skier's knees should be bent and forward so the plumb bob hangs directly over the front edge of the bootsole.

Four elements must be constant when this measurement is taken:

1. The skier must stand on a perfectly flat and level surface.

2. The skier's bootsoles must be parallel, and the feet in the width normally used for skiing. Measure this width so you can always repeat it.

3. The skier must flex the boot so the kneecap comes directly over the front edge of the bootsole.

4. The skier must look straight ahead, and stand in a relaxed, natural position.

Now hang the plumb–bob and measure where the skier's center of knee mass is relative to the center seam on the boot sole.

Next, with the skier continuing to face straight ahead, step to their side and look at their fore/aft stance. The center of their shoulder should be directly above the center of their bootsole. If not, note this for consideration when adjusting ramp angle, forward lean, or forward flex. (See photo 15.)

You are now ready to complete a preliminary alignment form. The information you'll need is shown in Form 1 on page 30. When this form is complete, you can proceed to the next step in the Balance Circle—building a footbed or orthotic.

Footnote (June 1994): It is *very* important that the issue of heel height be addressed as a part of building the footbed or orthotic. Unfortunately, few footbed or orthotic suppliers evaluate this need, or provide for it. If this is not done, proper balance and/or fit is difficult to attain regardless of what other adjustments are made to a skier's boots. This is one of the least understood issues in providing good balance for skiing.

How can you determine the heel height needed? You can be measured for equinus deformity by an orthopedic surgeon; or you can use this practical, self-help method: Stand barefoot on a level floor. Place an increasing number of pages of a magazine or book under your heels. Try 10 pages, 20 pages, 30 pages, etc. When you get the right number, your body will know. (The human body senses balance very precisely.) This is the heel lift you require. When you step off the magazine, your hips will drop and fall back, and you will feel "locked" in the "back seat."

The amount of heel lift that must be provided in your orthotic/footbed will depend on the shape of the ski boot footboard. *All* orthotics/footbeds must be custom fitted to each boot footboard they interface with.

Facing page: Alta skier, Molly Kissinger, shows good fore/aft alignment.

THE ATHLETIC SKIER
ASSESSMENT FORM

SKI SHOP _____

Evaluator _____

Customer:

   Name: _____   Phone: _____

   Address: _____

Boots: _____   Skis: _____

Footbed: _____   Orthotic: _____

Physician: _____   Pedorthist: _____

Unusual body build or special needs: _____

_____

_____

Center of knee mass marked on patellas? _____

What is the skiers tibia shape? _____

Does skier want footbed? _____   Orthotic? _____

If footbed exists, is it properly interfaced with the boot? _____

Amount of heel lift needed? _____

Where is forward lean set? _____

Where is forward flex set? _____

Will you be using the cuff for canting? _____

Is boot sole flat? Yes _____   No _____ If no, complete preliminary cant
evaluation to determine what part of the boot sole to plane.

Width of stance used for evaluation: _____

	SKIER'S LEFT KNEE			SKIER'S RIGHT KNEE	
Outside	*Inside*		*Outside*	*Inside*
_____	_____	-mm/inch-	_____	_____
_____	_____	-degrees-	_____	_____

What is the plan? _____

_____

_____

_____

_____

_____

_____

Chapter 4

FOOTBEDS AND ORTHOTICS

Nearly all skiers can benefit from a footbed or orthotic. The job of a **footbed** is to *support* the foot in a neutral position while in a ski boot. The job of an **orthotic** is not only to *support* the foot but also *to provide correction* to the foot so it maintains a neutral position in the boot.

Reducing available pronation to 2–6 degrees is the goal for 80 percent of skiers. Five to 15 degrees is common in most boots without a footbed. Pronation is the single most common factor in boot fit problems and in loss of energy transmission to the ski. (See photos 16 and 17.)

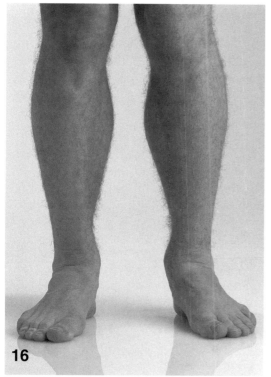

16

ERIK OSTLING

These are pronated feet standing relaxed on a flat floor. With the foot unsupported and poorly aligned, the forces common to skiing are misdirected to the inside of the arch.

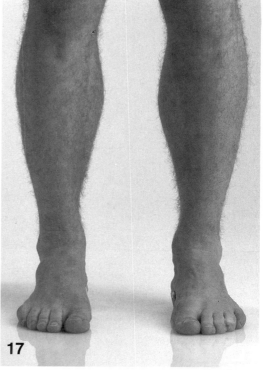

17

ERIK OSTLING

These are the same feet supported by a corrective orthotic. Notice how the tibia and foot are now aligned. This assures the forces of skiing will be transmitted evenly through the foot to the ski.

These photos show a pronated foot before and after correction. When in a skiing position, the forces that cause pronation are greatest. Almost all of us pronate excessively in a ski boot. Look at photo 16 and observe how the *knees are in, the arch is collapsed, and the feet are splayed out*. These are symptoms that 80 percent of skiers must deal with to varying degrees.

Loss of energy, through collapse of the foot and poor alignment, isn't the only problem associated with excessive pronation. Look again at drawing 2 (page 24) and photo 16. When the foot splays out and flattens in the boot, it puts excess pressure on the outside of the forefoot and the inside of the heel. How much larger does the unsupported foot look than the supported foot?

This movement of the foot inside the boot causes a wide variety of problems including: sixth toes, hammer toes, bone spurs, and blisters. In addition, nerve functions and blood flow are restricted. These cause cold feet and diminished functioning of balance receptors.

Five types of feet cause abnormal pronation: forefoot varus, forefoot valgus, rearfoot varus, tibia vara, and equinus deformity. These ten technically specific words should alert you that the building of footbeds and orthotics is the realm of trained professionals. We recommend you seek help from the best bootfitter, pedorthist, or podiatrist you can find.

Photo 18 shows feet that need lots of help. The left foot is supinated, and the right foot is pronated. It is not easily seen, but both feet suffer from equinus deformity and several other problems. Photo 19 shows these same feet on corrective orthotics. Notice how the feet are supported, the achilles tendons are now straight, and the legs are aligned. The extreme heel lifts you see are corrections for equinus deformity. Without this heel height correction, it would be very difficult for this skier to achieve fore/aft balance.

A good orthotic should always address the issue of heel height. Some makers of footbeds will do so as well. This is an important factor in fore/aft balance. Some people require no lift at all. Others need more than half an inch. If you don't have it right, fore/aft balance is hard to achieve. Skiers who purchase footbeds or orthotics should ask to have this issue addressed.

All footbeds must be custom fitted to the specific boot they are used in. In an ideal world, all boots would have flat surfaces to put footbeds or orthotics on. In the real world, the floor of every boot is different. On a lateral plane, some boots are flat, and others have 4 degrees of post. Two degrees is average; and many footboards are adjustable. It makes no sense to build a footbed on a flat floor, then install it on a posted footboard. Every footbed or orthotic must be shaped to rest in a specific boot without being deformed. For this reason footbeds cannot be moved from one boot to another without being interfaced with the new boot.

Throughout our years in skiing, we have seen a great number of abused feet. Some have been traumatized in ski boots; others are abused in everyday use. We wonder why people don't take better care of their feet. They get only one pair for a life-time of use.

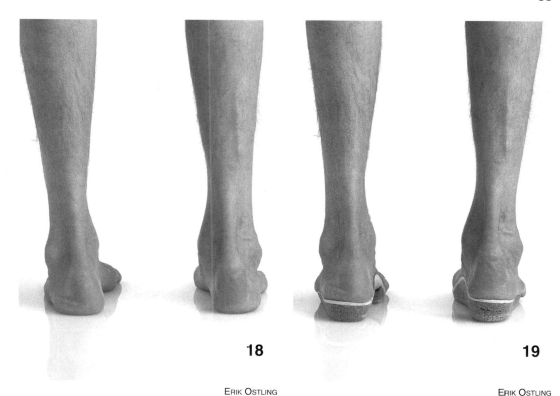

18

19

ERIK OSTLING

The left foot is supinated. The right foot is pronated.

ERIK OSTLING

With proper orthotics, both feet are well aligned. The extreme heel height is a correction for equinus deformity.

When training hard, athletes put enormous stresses on their feet. If they are hot and sore after hard workouts, ice and elevation will help them recover.

We recommend the use of orthotics in all athletic shoes, and for daily wear as well. They provide comfort, support, control, and protection from foot injuries. Good foot care helps your posture and contributes to your longevity as an athlete.

Chapter 5

FORE / AFT BALANCE

More than half the people we observe skiing are out of balance to the rear—some subtly, and others drastically. Whenever we do clinics for recreational skiers, we ask: "How many of you feel out of balance to the rear? Do you 'get in the back seat' and have to play catch up more often than you like?"

Three-fourths of our audience raise their hands. Many express frustration and ask for help. Every one of these skiers knows first hand the difficulty of skiing out of balance. They struggle with it every time they ski. One instructor said: "I've been in the back seat for ten years. I have always assumed it was one of my deficiencies as an athlete."

Like this instructor, most skiers blame *themselves* for their difficulties. They assume skiing is a hard sport and they haven't yet mastered it. They think when their technique improves they'll have better balance. In truth, ***its not their technique that's to blame. It's their boots.*** Boots can position a skier too far forward or too far back.

Boots *force* skiers out of balance to the rear in three ways: (1) the boot shaft is too vertical, (2) the boot is too stiff, (3) the footbed or ramp angle is too flat. Many skiers have all three of these factors working against them. If they tried to ice skate or in-line skate in a similar boot—they would fall over backward. They would know their boots didn't work, and would ask to change them. But skiers don't fall. Skiers can sit back and keep on going. They are saved by the phantom foot. (See drawing 5.)

"The Phantom Foot"

A snow ski provides a 2 to 3 foot platform in front of and behind the boot. When you step into skis, it's like having feet that are 6 feet long. This phantom foot provides wonderful fore/aft stability. When you ski and move dynamically, you can be way off balance and still not fall. This is how most people ski. With the phantom foot to lever against, their abdominal and other muscles work continuously to keep them upright. This isn't relaxed. It isn't efficient. It isn't balanced. But people accept it because they don't know any better. Now you know better. How can you fix it, and what do you need?

Photo 20 shows Armin Bittner skiing in excellent fore/aft balance. Look again at photo 4, and at other pictures of Karen Percy and Marc Girardelli. You need boots that allow you to ski in a similar stance. You need boots that allow your ankles to flex, your knees to flex, and your hips (center of mass) to be balanced over your boots.

The "PHANTOM FOOT"

5

DRAWING BY DIANE BODE

20

Thor Kellerud

Armin Bittner (GER) races slalom in a balanced position with his knees forward, his hips centered over his boots, and his torso erect. This position contributes to quickness and agility; and it allows the muscles of the lower back and abdomen to relax. Notice that Bittner does not reach forward with his arms or hunch his shoulders into a rounded position. Standing erect, with his shoulders back, allows him to bring his hips further forward and maintain balance over the middle of his skis.

To meet these needs, every person requires a slightly different boot. Your physical strength, the speed at which you ski, your body build and foot shape all affect the way a boot works. Boots must be matched to skiers. If you are purchasing new boots, a good bootfitter can help you get a good match. If you are adjusting old boots, or fine tuning new ones, you still need a bootfitter's help.

Please note that even when you have a suitable boot, it still requires fine tuning for *your* balance needs. It's a lucky customer who can buy new boots and ski in perfect balance without *substantial* custom fitting. For this reason, we encourage people to purchase boots at the best specialty shops—not at discount sporting goods stores (unless they have an experienced bootfitter on staff). ***If you save a dollar and lose your balance, you have paid a terrible price for your boots.*** What can a bootfitter do?

1. **Adjust the shaft angle.** Some boots have adjusting mechanisms built into the design. These are a wonderful help for bootfitting; but they don't always have enough adjustment to meet a skier's needs. Other boots require taking rivets out and re-attaching the cuff with more or less forward lean. New boots are available with forward lean ranging from 10 to 24 degrees. This wide range reveals how varied the needs of different skiers may be. It also suggests that *many* skiers are in boots that are far from ideal.

2. **Adjust the Flex.** Again, some boots have adjusting mechanisms built into the design. Good bootfitters can change the flex in a variety of ways. They can add or remove rivets in the back of the cuff. They can cut relief slots in the inner cuff. They can reduce friction of the closure straps. They can grind out excess material. This is a creative process with many options. Good bootfitters can do wonders with flex adjustment.

   Flex needs are closely related to the strength and style of a skier. Tomba's boots are unbelievably stiff; yet he flexes them with ease. He is incredibly strong and skis with speed and power. (See photo 53, page 122.) A hundred-pound intermediate skier has the same needs for range of motion as Tomba, but less force to achieve them with. A *much* softer boot is required. Most skiers fall somewhere between—which is why so many models are offered. Wanting "top of the line gear," many skiers buy boots that are too strong. The top line boots are made for aggressive, athletic skiers. They don't work for intermediates and beginners.

We observe many children and beginners skiing in boots too vertical and too stiff. They have little strength, and lack the skills to leverage forward in their boots. They wind up leaning back against the cuff—skiing with their knees over their heels and their hips far behind. It is incredibly difficult to progress in skiing from this position. Appropriate boots are needed to learn good skills. Some low-end boots are too soft in flex. These provide no support for skiers who press forward with their knees. Hence they must stand straight in the boot. If they then sit back, the soft boot doesn't support them there either; so they are left far in the back seat. These skiers are evident on every mountain. Finding just the right boot *is* a challenge. (See photo 21.)

21

Ashley Morse shows a position in which we see many children and adults. When there is no support for the back of the leg, skiers are left in a defensive posture, standing on their heels, and unable to use the front half of their skis. This slows the learning process for all skiers. If you look carefully at Ashley's left boot, you will see she has buckled it loosely so there is no support from the rear of the boot. If she buckled the boot more tightly, it would place her in a more productive stance. Many beginners, in rental boots, make this same mistake.

3. **Adjust ramp angle.** Look back to drawing 4 on page 26. This shows how every foot has a different need for heel height. If this need has been met with a proper footbed or orthotic, great. If not, *heel height must be addressed before changing the ramp angle.** Some skiers need a lift. Others do not.

*Please note that the heel height is different from ramp angle. Heel height affects the comfort and function of the foot, and also influences fore/aft balance. Changes in ramp angle affect fore/aft balance, but do not address the functional alignment of the foot.

New boots are available with ramp angles that vary from 2 to 7 degrees. Again, this is a broad range. (See drawing 6.)

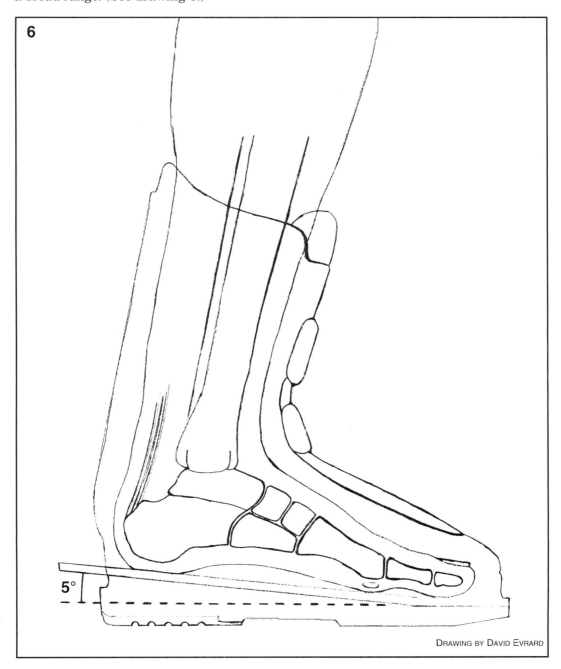

6

5°

DRAWING BY DAVID EVRARD

RAMP ANGLE

This boot has a five degree ramp angle.

To ski in perfect balance, you should have this angle right within a degree. If your body build requires 6 degrees, and you have a boot with 2, you have a *big* problem. If your boot has a 6 degree ramp and you need only 3, that's a problem too. You'll feel you are standing on a hill. Many new boots have ways to change the ramp angle built into the design. These are helpful, but often lack the range of adjustment required.

HEEL LIFTS OUTSIDE THE BOOT

Balance can also be changed on the fore/aft plane by using a heel lift *outside* the boot. In many cases this is the best way to achieve good balance. Unfortunately, modern binding designs don't easily accommodate heel lifts. Heel bindings are built for a specific sole thickness. Putting a lift under the heel binding changes the interface geometry at the toe. Bootfitters and balance specialists are denied a useful tool. A major binding company is working on a design that incorporates heel height adjustment. When available, it will be an aid to many skiers.

WHAT IS YOUR BODY BUILD?

More women than men are out of balance to the rear. Women, on average, carry more weight in their hips and less in their shoulders. Many race coaches think a majority of women skiers need a heel lift to ski in good balance.

People with long femurs are commonly out of balance to the rear. When they bend at the knees, their hips move further back than is common for people of average build. If you are tall, and have a footshape that requires a heel lift, you can't expect to be in balance in most boots. You need a bootfitter for a friend.

TECHNICAL INDICATIONS

There are many technical indications of fore/aft balance errors. The "back-seat" position is most obvious. People who bend too much at the waist are usually compensating for their hips being too far back. Some people carry their hands far in front of them. Others ski with their head thrust forward. If the center of mass is back, something else must move forward. The body instinctively seeks balance.

Look again at photos 1, 6, 10, and 11. Can you see how relaxed these skiers are? Stomach and lower back muscles don't have to maintain balance, or hold up a head that's too far forward. *These skiers show the position you want on your skis.* Other photos throughout this book support this image. If this isn't your stance, it's not your technique that's lacking. It's how your boots work. Fix them, and skiing becomes a whole lot easier and a lot more fun.

At this point, an astute reader might ask: "If so many skiers are out of balance to the rear, and the boots are to blame, why are ski boots designed as they are?" This is a good question; and one that bootmakers must answer. We believe that many boots for children and intermediates need more forward lean, a softer flex, and a steeper ramp angle. In high-end boots, a greater range of heel height adjustment is often needed.

Sometime in the late 80's, new DIN standards were set that caused binding manufacturers to raise their Anti-Friction Devices (on which the toe of the boot sits). Most AFDs are now 12–13 mm (1/2 inch) high. Not long ago, they were 4–8 mm. When the thickness of this toe support was increased, there was no equivalent rise in the height of the heel platform. For *all skiers* in the new bindings, the ramp angle of the boot sole was decreased; and they were tilted to the rear. A difference of just one degree in ramp angle has an enormous influence on balance—especially for the taller athlete. This little move in the ski industry went unnoticed by virtually all boot and binding manufacturers. Everyone's balance changed. No one took note.

Skiers should be aware that different bindings provide different ramp angles. A skier may be out of balance in binding A, and in balance in binding B. Another skier may have the opposite experience.

How do you know when you are in perfect fore/aft balance? Only through trial and error. When you find it you will know! Your abdominal, back, and leg muscles will relax. Your skeleton will carry your weight. You'll feel light, quick, and agile on your skis; and you'll have a smile on your face.

Footnote (June 1994): In our 1994 clinics with racers and ski instructors, we found that more than half were out of balance to the rear. A great many (especially the women) needed some heel lift inside the boot, where it should be integrated with the orthotic as discussed on pages 26 and 28.

Nearly all the young racers we worked with (ages 8-15) (and some National Team skiers as well) were handicapped by boots that were too stiff. There was a significant trend among World Cup racers in 1994 to use softer boots than they have chosen for the past few years. We applaud this trend. We urge younger racers to avoid most boots labeled "Junior Race" models. They are often too stiff. Better performances can be had with standard junior boots.

A woman instructor for whom we provided heel lifts said to us after making a dozen turns: "This is the first time in ten years of skiing that I feel my bones are stacked right." Our goal, for all skiers, is to help them "get their bones stacked right." This is a prerequisite for learning carving skills and becoming an athletic skier.

Chapter 6

BOOT CUFF ADJUSTMENTS

The adjustable cuff has been a welcome addition to boot designs. It provides all skiers an additional tool in the bootfitting process. Unfortunately, the cuff has been widely advertised as a "canting device." In truth, it is a proper canting device for only a small number of skiers who have a particular foot and leg shape.

CUFF ADJUSTMENT

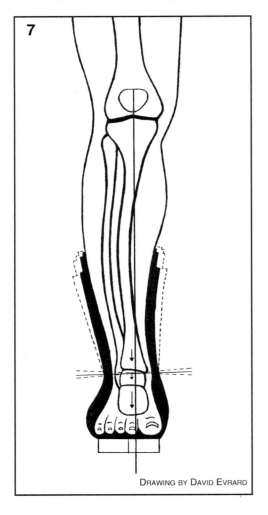

7

DRAWING BY DAVID EVRARD

For most skiers, the proper use of an adjustable cuff is to conform the boot cuff with the curve of their leg. This is the simplest part of the alignment process. (See drawing 7.)

The steps used to adjust the cuff are:

1. Remove liners from the boots.
2. Put the skier's footbeds or orthotics into the boots.
3. Have skier step into boots, and assume a natural skiing stance. (Be sure the footbed is in it's proper location.)
4. Adjust the cuff so the space between the leg and shell is equal on both sides.
5. Re-assemble boots and proceed with canting the skier (as outlined in the next chapter).

There are two situations where we recommend using the cuff for canting. These are appropriate for 10–20 percent of skiers. The first is when a bow-legged person has a pronated foot, and lots of tibia vara (curvature of the tibia) low in the leg. Moving the cuff inward will both reduce pronation and properly align the knee.

For most skiers the cuff should be adjusted so the leg is centered in the boot shaft. The foot and leg shown here are perfectly aligned. there is no pronation; and the knee is inside of center in the alignment that is most efficient for skiing. (See Chapter 7)

Before the cuff is adjusted (drawing 8), you can see both the pronation and the leg curve. After adjusting the cuff, as in drawing 9, we can see that the pronation is no longer apparent and the knee is in the position we would normally cant it. This skier can be properly aligned with a simple footbed, heel height adjustment, and boot cuff canting.

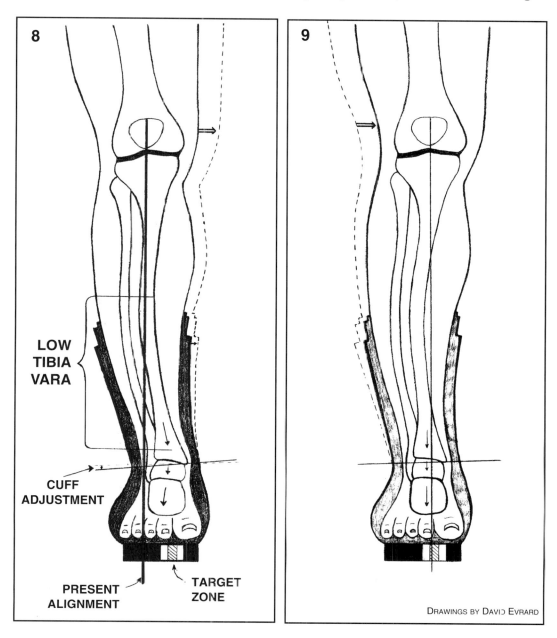

Before the cuff is adjusted, pronation is evident and the knee is aligned outside of center. After cuff adjustment, the pronation is reduced, and the knee is aligned in the 1–2 degree "Target Zone" inside of center.

The other situation (supination and tibial valgus) is rare. This is the opposite of the above situation. To picture it, visualize a knock-kneed person who has a very straight leg and a foot that rolls to the outside. We can adjust the cuff outward in this case. By doing so, the knee is properly aligned, and the forces which cause supination are reduced.

Whenever canting adjustments are made with the boot cuff, they should be followed with a canting evaluation as described in the next chapter. This will provide a final measurement of the knee position and, if necessary, a guide for making final canting adjustments outside the boot.

Chapter 7

CANTING / LATERAL BALANCE

If you look again at drawing 1 (The Alignment Circle), you will see that canting is the last step in the alignment process. An orthotic supports the foot in a neutral position. Fore/aft balance is provided. The boot cuff is set to conform to the leg shape. Now we cant—*under the bootsole—to provide a functional alignment of the leg bones that is best suited to the demands of skiing.*

WHY IS CANTING NECESSARY?

Only when properly canted can our bodies and skis work as efficiently as possible. By tilting or canting our boots, we can precisely control the geometry of our legs and establish an ideal position over our skis.

If the forces in alpine skiing were primarily vertical, the most efficient alignment of the knee would be centered directly over the foot. Skiers, however, must cope with centrifugal forces. To anticipate and gain leverage over these forces, skiers need a mechanical advantage at the beginning of turns.

Angulation provides this advantage. The quickest and easiest angulation is achieved by placing the knee to the inside of a turn—*before the turn begins.* We must, therefore, be slightly "knock-kneed" when riding a flat ski.

HOW KNOCK-KNEED SHOULD WE BE?

Nearly all skiers should be canted so their knees are between 1 and 2.5 degrees inside of vertical when their skis are flat. This is equivalent to "undercanting," or moving the knee inside by 1/4 to 3/4 of an inch. Achieving this position is the goal of canting.(See "Ideal Alignment" in photos 22B, 23B, and 24B.)

These photos of Tina Vindum show her in three stances: "Bow Legged," "Ideal," and Knock-Kneed." If different boots put her in each of these positions *when her skis are flat,* she would *over edge, edge efficiently,* or *under edge.* The mechanical advantage of the ideal stance is evident in these pictures. To trained observers, it is equally evident on snow. Imagine starting all of your turns from the three positions Tina demonstrates. Which would be most efficient and most comfortable? Which would be most difficult?

Which photos of Tina best represent the position of your knees when you stand in your ski boots, *with the soles flat on the floor?*

KNEE ALIGNMENT
(WHEN BOOT SOLES ARE FLAT)

Knees Out	Knees 1° – 2.5° Inside [1/4 – 3/4 inch]	Knees 2.5° + Inside
Bow-Legged	Slight Angulation	Knock-Kneed

Eric Ostling

OVER-CANTED	IDEAL ALIGNMENT	UNDER-CANTED

KNEE ALIGNMENT
(WHEN BOOT SOLES ARE FLAT)

Knees Out	Knees 1° – 2.5° Inside [1/4 – 3/4 inch]	Knees 2.5° + Inside
Bow-Legged	Slight Angulation	Knock-Kneed

ERIC OSTLING

OVER-CANTED	IDEAL ALIGNMENT	UNDER-CANTED

KNEE ALIGNMENT
(WHEN BOOT SOLES ARE FLAT)

Plumb-bob is outside of center line	Plumb-bob is 1° – 2.5° inside of center line	Plumb-bob is more than 2.5° inside of center line

24A **24B** **24C**

OVER-CANTED	IDEAL ALIGNMENT	UNDER-CANTED

TECHNICAL INDICATIONS FOR CANTING

OVER-CANTED (Bow-legged)	IDEAL ALIGNMENT (1°–2.5° Inside)	UNDER-CANTED (Knock-kneed)
Poor angulation. Head leans in. Hip stays outside.	**Uses Knee and hip angulation in natural proportion.**	Uses excessive knee angulation.
Turns begin with lateral push of ski, or a pronounced stem.	**Turns begin with minimum lateral push or skid of outside ski.**	Ski slides at beginning of turn. Loses edge hold and skids in sustained turns.
Skis are "grabby" and over-turn.	**Carving skills are easy and natural. Turns begin with edge and pressure.**	Skiers are limited to skidded turns. They have insufficient edge for carving.
Ski responds too quickly.	**Ski responds "delightfully."**	Ski responds too slowly.
Quickness and agility are limited by poor balance and muscle tension.	**Quickness and agility are enhanced by good balance, relaxation, and solid edge platform of carving ski.**	Quickness and agility are limited by skidding ski and lack of edge platform.
Downhill knee wobbles in and out.	**Harmony of angulation, edge angle, and balance reduces chattering and skidding.**	Knees always inside, often bang together. Skis slide on hard snow.
Tired quads. Muscles and joints are always under tension.	**Relaxed stance. Does not tire easily.**	Soreness and bruising on inside of knees.

Can you find a description of *your* skiing in this chart? Does it conform to your observed leg shape and knee alignment?

The photos of Bow-legged Mike and Knock-kneed Andy on the next two pages show how changing knee alignment affects technique.

BOW-LEGGED MIKE

25A   25B

Byron Hetzler

Photos 25A and 25B: *Mike has been skiing for 25 years. He is naturally bow-legged. With his ski boots on, his natural stance is similar to that shown by Tina in photos 22A, 23A, and 24A. His downhill ski is thus severely over edged; he cannot use appropriate knee angulation; and he skis with a stiff lower leg to keep his outside ski from over-turning. (See photo A.) This stiff leg is Mike's defense against wobbly knee syndrome.*

After cants are placed under Mike's bindings (thick side outside to move his knees in), his stance changes immediately. (See photo B.) He is now able to use knee angulation to control edging. He can flex his knees, and stand balanced over his downhill ski. After 25 years, no amount of technical coaching could significantly improve Mike's skiing. A simple adjustment in his knee alignment, however, has a dramatic impact. Mike is now more relaxed, more efficient, and more balanced. He can learn to carve turns, which was nearly impossible in his old stance. Most important, Mike's pleasure in skiing has been greatly enhanced by proper knee alignment.

Photos 26A and 26B: *Andy is an aggressive and powerful skier who has extensive racing experience. He can ski all terrain with control and grace. Most skiers would be thrilled to ski as well. Why should we consider changing the alignment of so good a skier? Because we can help him to ski better; and he wants to improve.*

Andy's problem is a knock-kneed stance similar to that shown by Tina in photos 22C, 23C, and 24C. To gain the edging he needs, Andy must ski in a more flexed knee position and with more angulation than is most efficient. Photo A shows that Andy's legs form a pronounced "A-frame" from his knees to his boots. A 1-2.5 degree A-frame is good. This is too much.

After fitting cants under Andy's bindings (thick side inside to move his knees out), the A-frame is reduced, and his stance is more erect. (photo B)

Viewed from the side at the end of a turn, we see Andy again when undercanted in photo C, and when properly aligned in photo D. When knock-kneed, Andy needed a low hip position to provide greater knee angulation and hence more edge. When properly canted, his stance is taller, more relaxed, and offers a greater range of motion.

KNOCK-KNEED ANDY

26A 26B

BYRON HETZLER

26C 26D

BYRON HETZLER

The majority of skiers we observe on the hill or test in our laboratory are over-canted. They stand bow-legged when their skis are flat on the snow. To appreciate how this affects technique, try this simple exercise:

While sitting in a chair, relax and place your feet flat on the floor, about 6 inches apart. Move your knees 12 inches apart. Imagine you have skis and boots on. Now try to apply edge angle and pressure to the inside edge of your right ski. Is this an efficient movement?

It is difficult to pressure the inside edge when your knee is outside of vertical. Your knee must first rise and move inward until it passes over the top of its arc. Only when the knee reaches a position inside of vertical, can you effectively apply pressure *down* onto the inside edge.

Next, try the same exercise starting with your feet 6 inches apart and your knees 5 inches. From this slightly knock-kneed position, can you more easily apply pressure directly to the inside edge? Yes. When you are properly canted, you experience this same efficiency in your skiing.

The lateral position of the knee plays a major role in determining the amount of edge angle a skier has at all stages of a turn. *Proper canting assists in the smooth initiation of turns, and places a skier in the most balanced and powerful stance throughout a turn.*

All errors in canting geometry are reflected in a skier's technique. Please study the chart on page 49; and look ahead to drawings 18 A, B, and C on pages 170–171.

In the "Technical Indications of Canting" chart, each column describes how people ski *because of their alignment.* ***For the bow-legged and knock-kneed stances, each "mistake" in skiing is not a failure of the skiers' athleticism; it's an error FORCED on skiers by their boots.***

Most readers will find accurate descriptions of their skiing somewhere on this chart. We hope it's in the second column; but only a lucky few are skiing in this alignment. Let's look at the three most common problems we see on the ski hill. All are in column one, and are caused by being over-canted, or over-edged.

1. **Poor angulation / Head leans in / Hip stays outside.** These body positions are especially evident in the initial phase of a turn; but they are seen through the belly of a turn as well. If a skier in this alignment were to use efficient knee angulation, his skis would be *over-edged,* and would turn too sharp. *The best instructor in the world can't teach proper angulation to an over-canted skier.* If a good bootfitter provides proper alignment to this skier, then good angulation will occur naturally. ***Many technical problems are solved more easily in the boot shop than in ski school.*** Only after alignment needs are met, can instructors teach (or students learn) athletic skiing.

2. **Turns begin with a lateral push of the outside ski, or with a pronounced stem.** This skier cannot begin a turn with subtle and balanced knee angulation. The ski edges too much if the knee is moved inside. The ski must be pushed away from the body so the skier has more leverage against it and can better control the excess edge. This turn always begins with a heel push and skid.

3. **Downhill knee wobbles in and out.** We call this the "wobbly knee syndrome." It's most evident in the middle of a turn on hard snow. It is the surest sign of a skier whose downhill ski is too much on edge.

This skier tries to maintain knee angulation because that is the most comfortable, strong, and relaxed position for skiing. When the knee moves in, the ski is over-edged and turns too sharp. To take the ski off edge, the knee must move out. Thus, a constant battle is waged. The leg, trying to provide good balance, says: "Angulate." The ski shouts: "Take me off edge, I'm over-turning." And the poor, tired knee wobbles in and out looking for a harmony it can never find. At days end, the knee is sore and the supporting muscles are tired and stiff.

Do you see yourself in these descriptions? Or a friend you ski with? Who is to blame for the difficulties an improperly canted skier has to cope with? *Nearly all skiers blame themselves*—or their lack of technique and coordination.

The Blame Game

It's human nature to blame yourself for failure in sports. In baseball, if you swing at a pitch and miss, it's your fault, not the bat's. In basketball, if you shoot and miss, that's your fault too. In skiing, if your turns are awkward or you're not improving, it's again human nature to blame yourself. This is humble, but not wise. We call it *"the blame game."*

Skiing is different from all other sports—because the boot determines so much of our balance and stance. Every indication of poor skiing on our technical chart is caused by poor alignment. Skiers who play "the blame game" will always be frustrated and handicapped. Those who change their alignment, like Bow-Legged Mike and Knock-Kneed Andy, will enjoy immediate and long term improvements in their skiing.

In a perfect world, all skiers will complete steps 1–4 on the alignment circle before addressing canting needs. Realistically, we know that many skiers haven't the time or money to purchase orthotics or have other professional work done on their boots. For these skiers, *proper canting—done with whatever boots they have—provides large gains in skiing performance.*

There are two steps in canting. First, determine your canting need. Second, provide the necessary "fix."

HOW TO DETERMINE CANTING NEEDS

Follow these steps to determine canting needs.

(Fill in Canting Evaluation Form as you proceed.)

1. If you have orthotics or footbeds, be certain they are properly interfaced with your boot.

2. Remove from the boot any tape, padding, or shims previously installed to achieve a canting goal. Leave padding that improves fit.

3. If available, adjust boot cuff as described in Chapter 6.

4. Complete all other boot fitting procedures.

5. Make sure that bootsoles are perfectly flat, not warped or excessively worn. A simple test is to set a boot on a flat surface, tip it a few degrees on edge, and let it rock back to center. If the soles are flat and parallel, the boot settles quickly in place. If the boots are warped or worn, the boot rocks gently back and forth.

   If necessary, true the soles with a belt sander or planer. This procedure requires special skills and equipment not widely available. We understand the difficulties; but we insist that flat soles improve both binding and ski performance. The ski industry must address this issue.

6. Wear shorts or other clothing that allows the knee to be exposed, and doesn't pull your skin in any direction.

7. With a pen, draw a vertical line **on the center of knee mass** on each knee. (See photo 13, page 23.) A discriminating eye and good judgement are required here. **Be precise.**

8. Assume a normal skiing stance, *with feet parallel*, on a *flat*, *hard*, and *level* floor. (Check it carefully with a carpenter's level). We suggest you identify a specific place in your shop that you are certain is level, and use this space for all canting evaluations. A marked grid makes it easy to keep boots parallel and to measure stance width. Record the distance between the skier's boots so you can duplicate it for subsequent evaluations. See recommended "Cant Evaluation Form" on opposite page.

9. Bend your knees until they move as far forward as the front of your boot sole. Then move each knee slightly left and right—rocking the boot sole from one edge to the other—until certain the soles are flat on the floor.

   Hang a plumb-bob (available at hardware stores) from the knee center-line to the front edge of the boot sole. Mark the boot where the plumb-bob indicates. (See photo 14, page 27; and photos 24 A,B,C.)

THE ATHLETIC SKIER
CANTING EVALUATION FORM

SKI SHOP _____

Evaluator _____

Customer:

Name: _____ Phone: _____

Address: _____

Boots: _____ Skis: _____

Bindings: _____ Footbeds: _____

Orthotics: _____ Skier ability: _____

Are Orthotics or Footbeds properly interfaced with boots? Left _____ Right _____

Unusual body build or special needs: _____

_____

Are boot soles flat? Left _____ Right _____ (If no, complete preliminary cant evaluation to determine which side of the boots should be ground to level the sole).

Grind Left Boot   (inside edge _____) (outside edge _____).

Grind Right Boot (inside edge _____) (outside edge _____).

Width of Stance used for evaluation (_____).

Knee Center-Line marked on (Patella _____) or (adjusted _____).

SKIER'S RIGHT KNEE				**SKIER'S LEFT KNEE**		
Outside	*Neutral*	*Inside*		*Outside*	*Neutral*	*Inside*
_____	_____	_____	-mm/inch-	_____	_____	_____
_____	_____	_____	-degrees-	_____	_____	_____

CANT REQUIRED _____   CANT REQUIRED _____

Move Knee   IN_____OUT_____   Move Knee   IN _____OUT_____

TO MOVE KNEE IN — MOUNT WEDGE OR CANT THICK SIDE OUTSIDE!

TO MOVE KNEE OUT — MOUNT WEDGE OR CANT THICK SIDE INSIDE!

FINAL MEASUREMENTS

Right Boot Toe	**Left Boot Toe**
_____	_____
_____	_____

[Recommended Stance is between 1 and 2.5 degrees inside.]

[Exception: extremely bow-legged skiers whose natural stance is more than 3° outside]

A carpenter's framing square can also be used. Place the short end flat on the floor and align its vertical long end with the mark on the knee center-line. Mark the boot where the vertical edge crosses the sole.

10. Measure the distance of this mark from the raised casting line that indicates the exact center of the boot sole. This measurement reveals how far inside or outside of vertical the knee is in a skiing stance. (See photo 27.) Use the Canting Conversion Chart (opposite) to convert distance measurements to degrees of cant.

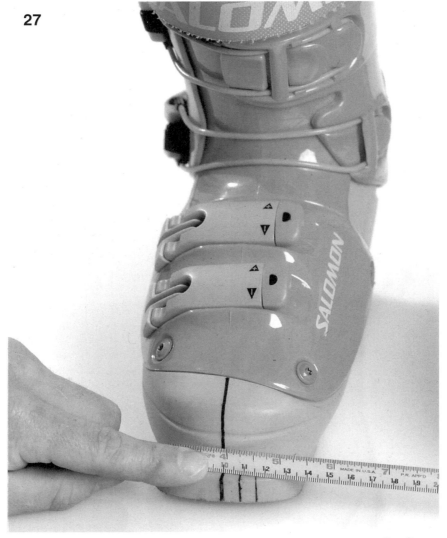

27

Measure the distance the knee is displaced from the center-line; then use the **Canting Conversion Chart** *to convert distance to degrees. Please note that leg length must be considered for all conversions.*

CANTING CONVERSION CHART

(Distance Measure to Degrees)

DEGREES OF CANT	1°	2°	3°	4°
Knee Displacement for knee height 16"*	7 mm 1/4"	14 mm 9/16"	21 mm 13/16"	28 mm 1 1/8"
Knee Displacement for knee height 18"	8 mm 5/16"	16 mm 5/8"	24 mm 15/16"	32 mm 1 1/4"
Knee Displacement for knee height 20"	9 mm 11/32"	18 mm 11/16"	27 mm 1 1/16"	36 mm 1 3/8"
Knee Displacement for knee height 22"	10 mm 3/8"	20 mm 3/4"	30 mm 1 3/16"	40 mm 1 1/2"
Thickness of a wedge for bootsole 69 mm wide	1.2 mm	2.4 mm	3.6 mm	4.8 mm
Thickness of a wedge for binding 58 mm wide	1.0 mm	2.0 mm	3.0 mm	4.0 mm

WE RECOMMEND THE KNEES BE FROM 1° to 2.5° INSIDE FOR MOST SKIERS.

*Measure from floor to knee with boots on.

There is no perfect angle of canting that can be established for any skier in the boot lab or ski shop. We recommend that bootfitters set most skiers 1.5 degrees inside. This provides a "functional and efficient stance" that is within one degree of optimum for skiers with "normal" legs. For performance skiers who require the utmost precision, final canting evaluations must be done on snow. Optimum canting for high performance skiing will vary slightly depending on individual body builds, skis used, boots used, the manner in which ski bases are prepared, snow conditions, and the specific task of the skier.

Most skiers will measure differently on their left and right legs. It is common to find a variance of 5 to 10 mm or 3/16 to 3/8 of an inch.

If a knee is inside of vertical from 1 to 2.5 degrees (See photos of "Ideal Stance"), a skier is well aligned and can ski efficiently on that leg.

If a knee is outside of center, or less than 1 degree inside (See photos of "Bow-Legged" stance), the skier requires a canting wedge under the outside of the boot sole. This tilts the boot and the knee inward.

If a knee is more than 2.5 degrees inside (See photos of "Knock-Kneed" stance), the skier requires a canting wedge under the inside edge of the boot sole. This tilts the boot and the knee outward.

Remember:

> TO MOVE THE KNEE IN—PLACE A CANT THICK SIDE OUTSIDE.
>
> TO MOVE THE KNEE OUT—PLACE A CANT THICK SIDE INSIDE.

Nearly all skiers turn better on one leg than the other. They assume this is caused by some fault in technique ("the blame game" again). In most cases the "bad leg" is simply the one with the greatest canting need.

No one can tell the exact leg geometry that will work best for each individual. Our experience shows that having the knees inside from 1 to 2.5 degrees works best for almost all skiers. Some may prefer closer to vertical (but seldom outside); and a few will ski best as far as 3 degrees inside. Optimal canting may differ for the left and right leg.

Chapters 28 and 33 provide additional information on fine tuning canting needs through experimentation on snow.

Skiers who are exceedingly bowlegged have special problems. We do not recommend canting a person more than 3 degrees except in special circumstances. See note page 59.*

MEETING CANTING NEEDS

When you have carefully determined your canting need—there are five ways to cant your boots. All work *under the boot sole*.

1. Interchangeable, canted soles offer the quickest and most economical method of addressing canting needs. Unfortunately, only DaleBoots and some Salomon models now offer this feature. We expect additional manufacturers will provide canted soles when the original patent expires in 1995.

2. Place a cant, or wedge, under the binding. This is the classic method of achieving large changes in canting needs. If installed in a professional manner, with screws

appropriately sized for cant thickness, cants placed under a binding do not affect binding release functions.

3. For racers and others who use multiple pairs of skis, sanding or planing the soles is the best option. Because this fix is a permanent part of the boot, a skier can select any pair of skis and always be perfectly canted. A full degree of cant is often achievable in this way as a part of flattening a warped boot sole. After boot soles are sanded, the top edge of the sole should be built up on the thin side until the original sole thickness is obtained. This assures the bootsole conforms to DIN standards. (Toe 19mm ±1; Heel 30mm ±1.)

4. To effect small canting changes (1 degree or less), it's easy to place plastic tape under one side of a binding. Loosen the binding screws. Apply tape (between the binding and the ski) in 3/4-inch width, and tighten binding. (See photo 71, page 188.) This does not in any way affect binding function or release settings. Six strips of Scotch Decorate and Repair Tape (available at office supply stores) will provide 1 degree of cant.

5. For skiers with the particular physiology discussed in Chapter 6, proper canting can be achieved by adjusting the boot cuff. For all other skiers, boot cuff adjustment is not the best way to meet canting needs. If the boot cuff has been used, check the final knee alignment by the same procedures listed in this chapter.

Proper canting improves skiing performance. It must become an accepted part of boot fitting. ***Canting is the final step in the alignment process that makes efficient and balanced skiing possible for all skiers.***

The steps presented here will place nearly all skiers within 1 degree of optimum alignment. Finer canting evaluations must be done by trial and error *on snow*. Readers who wish to proceed to the most precise canting adjustments, will find additional procedures in the special sections for instructors and racers.

Very good skiers, who are particularly sensitive to alignment needs, can feel changes as small as 1/8 of a degree. This is equivalent to an angle change created by a single piece of D and R tape. Racers should cant to this standard of accuracy. All good skiers who seek optimum performance should cant to an accuracy of 1/4 degree.

*Note for extremely bow-legged skiers: The canting procedures and alignment goals presented here are effective for more than 90% of all skiers. Special considerations are required for bow-legged skiers whose canting needs are greater than 3 degrees. If this extreme morphology exists, it is often unwise to move the knees inside of center. For skiers in the 3°–4° range, about 50 percent can be canted by moving the knee in. For the other 50 percent, it is most helpful to mount the cant thick side inside and provide a flat ski when they stand in their normal bow-legged stance. This choice must be made based on joint spaces and flexibility in the knee. Individual analysis and expert guidance are recommended for people with this leg shape. It is often wise to consult an orthopedic specialist. Nearly all bow-legged skiers who require more than 4° of cant are best served by mounting the cant thick side inside and providing a flat ski. The advantages of skiing with the knees 1°–2.5° inside of center are not attainable for extremely bow-legged persons.

Chapter 8

80/20 : 20/80

W hen you change your fore/aft balance or your canting—

The first 80 percent of correction provides a 20 percent gain in performance.

The last 20 percent of correction provides an 80 percent gain in performance!

If you are way in the back seat, and you move up to a little in the back seat, *you are still in the back seat*. Out of balance is out of balance. A little bit out of balance isn't much better than a lot.

If you are way over-canted, and you move to a little over-canted, *you are still over-canted*. You'll still push your skis at the start of a turn, and still lean in with your head.

In our first description of an athletic skier, we said our goal was *perfect balance*; and "good balance" was never good enough. The 80/20 equation explains why "perfect" balance is our goal. When we say this, we are not being "alignment fanatics" or techno-geeks. The 80/20 equation is the simple, practical truth of balance and alignment in skiing.

In gymnastics, on the balance beam, if you lose your balance just a little, you fall the same distance as when you lose it a lot. In skiing, if you are off balance just a little, your phantom foot prevents you from falling; but your skiing suffers a lot. Trust us. There are no shortcuts. Success requires precision.

This is a small chapter, but a big idea. You have to get it perfect. *It's the last 20 percent that offers the greatest reward.*

Chapter 9

THE PHYSIOLOGY OF BALANCE

I t is helpful for athletes to know how their bodies work. The physiology of balance explains the relationships between balance, muscle recruitment, and nerve functions. Our bodies have many more balance sensing mechanisms than our eyes and ears. Every muscle and every joint space is full of proprioceptors. These are nerve tissues that tell us where our bodies are located in space. Proprioception helps our joints keep track of their relationships to each other. Their success in this task significantly affects balance. Our feet, and particularly the soles of our feet, have a disproportionately large number of proprioceptors in them. Skiers should think of their feet as the third most important balance center in their bodies.

There are three ways we can enhance the balance work our feet must do:

1. Keep them free from tension.
2. Keep them as free as possible from compression.
3. Keep them warm.

Tension: Tension affects both nerve and muscle efficiency. Nerves function like phone cables. They can carry only so many signals at a time (See drawing 10.)

NERVE PATHWAYS

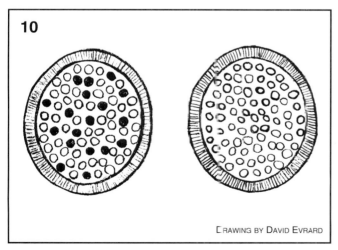

10

CRAWING BY DAVID EVRARD

The image on the left shows a nerve that is partially busy. When an athlete's natural stance is out of balance, some muscles and their accompanying nerves are always under tension. The dark dots represent nerve pathways that are busy providing balance. Only the clear pathways are free to respond to performance demands. An athlete's quickness, agility, balance, strength, and cordination are reduced in proportion to the nerve pathways that are occupied by balancing tasks.

The image on the right shows a nerve with all its pathways clear. This nerve can provide full muscle recruitment to an athlete. It can support optimum performance.

Whenever "compensatory balancing conversations" are going on, muscle recruitment is diminished in direct proportion to the number of nerve pathways occupied by balancing tasks.

Efficient muscle activation requires a preparatory stretch and a microsecond of complete neural silence. Good balance provides both. Muscles that are working to sustain balance are tense, are not able to pre-stretch, and have no "silence." When their nerve pathways are partially occupied with balancing tasks, they cannot fire completely. Thus, tension (which is caused by poor balance) both slows and weakens athletic performance.

Compression: Compression inhibits balance in two ways. First, a compressed nerve, like a tense one, can't carry all the signals it is normally able to. Second, compression restricts blood flow. In a skiing environment, cold tissues result. A skier's feet, compressed into plastic boots, are especially vulnerable. (See drawing 11.)

Nerves carry information in two directions *simultaneously*—both to and from the central nervous system. The CNS must know a muscle's position before it can provide a useful response. When nerve and circulatory systems are compressed and cold, communication to the CNS slows down. Complex athletic movements require fast integrative processing by the CNS. If one side of the information flow is slowed or stopped, the opposite side is equally slowed.

Warmth: Our bodies function like a zoned heating system. This system has clear priorities. The body core and brain come first. The arms and legs are second. The hands and feet come last. When we lose too much heat, circulation to the hands and feet is turned off. Cold ensues, and balance is compromised.

Low temperatures inhibit motion in two ways. First, since muscle fibers work electrochemically, and chemical reactions are slowed by low temperatures, muscles are slower when cold. Second, since nerves work on the same electrochemical principles, they also are slowed by cold. Cold nerves provide slow communication to muscle tissues. Warm nerves provide quick communication.

The best way to understand this slow down is to remember a time when you came indoors with cold hands and tried to write a letter, play the piano, or use a computer keyboard. Your fingers didn't work well. When cold, every muscle and nerve in your body suffers a comparable slow down.

Both basic science and practical experience tell us that quickness, agility, and balance are inhibited by cold. What percent of normal function do we lose?

John Higgins research at the University of Utah shows the following: ***For each 18-degree (F) drop in foot temperature, balance performance decreases by 12 percent.*** These figures were derived in controlled laboratory settings. His on-snow tests

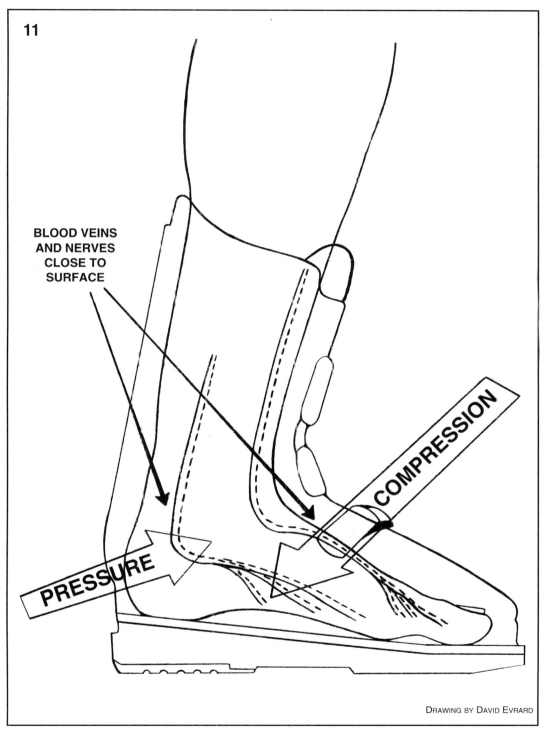

BLOOD VEINS
AND NERVES
CLOSE TO
SURFACE

COMPRESSION

PRESSURE

DRAWING BY DAVID EVRARD

Wherever ski boots compress the foot, nerve functions and blood flow are diminished. This drawing shows the areas that are most susceptible to compression. Boots must provide firm support; but they must do so without inhibiting circulation and nerve communication.

revealed that on a day when the temperature was 20 degrees, feet that averaged 86 degrees indoors cooled to 67 degrees after two hours of skiing.

Six of the skiers in this experiment were racers with close-fitting boots. Their feet cooled to 40 degrees. Clearly they were fitting and buckling their boots tighter than recreational skiers. What price were they paying?

A 46-degree temperature loss in the foot impairs balance by 30 percent. For racers, striving for hundredths of a second in time, this is a huge loss. We were surprised when confronted with these numbers. They explain why many World Cup racers have heaters in their boots.

In Chapters 3–8, we focused on how ski boots affect balance through alignment. Now we see that boot *fit* affects balance in other ways. When a good orthotic supports the foot and allows it to relax, more nerve pathways are open and better balance results. The support of the orthotic also lets skiers buckle their boots more loosely. Compression of the foot is reduced, so balance is again improved.

When you understand how nerve pathways work, you can see that skier alignment helps balance in two ways: One, it places our bodies in the most efficient position for skiing. And two, this position allows muscles to relax so nerve pathways are free and balancing information can be quickly processed. One aid to balance serves another. Quickness, agility, and strength are enhanced; and we ski better. That's our goal.

Chapter 10

AVAILABILITY OF SERVICES

Most skiers will require the help of an experienced bootfitter to accomplish the alignment goals set forth in the previous five chapters. Are qualified personnel available? And if so, what services will they provide? There is good news and bad.

GOOD NEWS

The United States leads the world in providing boot-related services. There are more than two thousand experienced bootfitters working in ski and specialty shops nationwide. They take pride in their work. They combine mechanical skills, an understanding of feet, and considerable ingenuity to provide comfort and fit to their customers. As we write, they are making footbeds for nearly half of new boot purchasers, and for thousands of customers with old boots and abused feet.

BAD NEWS

Few bootfitters or ski shop technicians are well trained to understand *the whole suspension system* and its effect on skier performance. They are good at boots. They are not tuned in to skier alignment and canting needs.

Most ski and boot shops simply do not address canting issues. They size boots. They provide footbeds (but seldom address the heel height required). They adjust forward lean, flex, and cuffs on boots with those options. But, when all of this is done, ***they hardly ever check canting needs***.

We are convinced that canting must be the final step in the alignment process. In the real world—in 1993—***canting is the neglected step in 99 percent of bootfitting procedures.***

In the bootfitter's defense, little education has been available on canting. Ski instructors have never been trained to play the role appropriate for them in helping their students and working with ski shops. Concerns over liability have scared some shops from mounting cants under the bindings. Longer screws for this process are difficult to acquire.

The obstacles to working with canting have been greater than the ski industry's commitment to it. Boot and binding manufacturers have been focused on other issues: DIN standards for soles and binding interfaces, release and retention capability in bindings, litigation concerns, marketing, and just surviving in a recession.

MORE GOOD NEWS.

Can we expect a growing attention to alignment issues and the "suspension system" in the future? Yes! Most of the problems listed above have been solved. The ski industry is now at a point where it can pay more attention to skier performance. Salomon engineers say: "We have nearly reached the limit on improving the release and retention capability of our bindings. Our research is now directed toward skier performance." This is a wonderful point of view, and one that's spreading in the ski industry.

The DaleBoot/Salomon patent on cantable soles expires in 1995. Numerous boot companies are already working on the options that will soon be available. In a few years we expect a wide selection of boots with cantable soles. There should also be bindings as easily adjustable for lateral canting and heel height as for boot retention. When canting and heel height are easier to experiment with, millions of skiers will be able to improve their alignment and their skiing.

While waiting for these advances, skiers must demand traditional canting services from ski shops and bootfitters. Canting materials *are* available.* All of the major binding companies *do approve* of mounting cants under their bindings—"if done in a professional manner, with appropriate screws, and allowing proper function of the brake, etc." With the knowledge in this book, skiers and bootfitters can make giant steps forward in providing alignment services.

We especially encourage bootfitters and instructors to educate themselves and become "alignment specialists". There is a potentially huge demand for good service to skiers both on the hill and in the shop. ***Bootfitters should consider becoming Board Certified Pedorthists. For those with a little ambition, there are opportunities for a substantial income and year-round employment.*** The ski industry needs these services.**

In closing, we'd like to return to the concept of the Alignment Circle on page 22. It's best to follow all steps in this circle. If limited by time or funds, it's still productive to follow as many steps as you can. Each step leads to better skiing. Anyone can measure their canting needs at home with a friend, a plumb-bob, and a ruler. Find out where you are. Then decide where you are going and whose help you will need. If you are one of the 90 percent of skiers who have an alignment handicap, get ready for big improvements in your skiing when you fix them.

*Canting strips, screw kits, and the cant evaluator pictured on page 174 are manufactured by The Cant Co., and are distributed to the ski industry by Spirakut, P.O. Box 3430, Hailey, Idaho 83333. Phone (800) 621-1657.

**For information on pedorthist certification, contact The Prescription Footwear Association, 9861 Brokenhand Parkway, Suite 265, Columbia, MD 21046-1151. (800) 673-8447.

PART 3

THE SKI

A modern snow ski is the eighth wonder of the world. It carves turns in 4 feet of powder, through 2 feet of crud, or on ice you can skate on. It carries your weight, accelerates when you wish, and stops when you tell it to. It rides over bumps and steers through ruts. If you're a good enough skier, it earns you a living.

WOW! It's a wonderful tool. If you edge it, pressure it, and steer it—in just the right ways—it will turn as you wish. How does it work?

We wish there was space to tell how skis are made—and why they work as they do. These are fascinating subjects. Those who are interested should read *The Ski Handbook: A Compilation of Information on the Technical Aspects of Skis*.* Two paragraphs from this book help us to understand the goals of ski designers.

> . . . the interaction between bending, twist, camber, and sidecut determine a skier's weight distribution onto the snow when turning. The trick is to blend these properties to provide a **control feel**. *The feel of the whole edge carving on the snow and working in a turn is the trademark of an outstanding ski.*" (Our italics.)

> . . . the new equipment gives the Mahres and Tomba better ski control than their predecessors. This allows them to be more precise, go straighter at the turns, and turn more sharply while preserving speed. For recreational skiers, the bottom line is that we can be more subtle in our edge settings and more effective in our applications of front/back pressures. . . . *We can carve rather than skid our turns and skiing is easier and more graceful.* (Our italics.)

Virtually all ski manufacturers are working to make skis that "carve rather than skid," and make skiing "easier and more graceful." From our perspective, *the designers have produced extraordinary skis*; but too few skiers have learned how to use them. Racers, and other athletic skiers, have learned. That's clear from the pictures in this book. Other skiers, who haven't learned carving, are missing the fun. They have bought Porches, and are running them on two cylinders.

Wonderful skis are available to all. Let's learn how to use them.

* *THE SKI HANDBOOK* (48pp) is available from K2 Race Department, K2 Corporation, Vashon Island, WA 98070. ($10.00) This fascinating book is easily understood by lay readers.

Chapter 11

THE UTILIZATION OF SKI DESIGN

When gliding forward, if you roll a ski on edge and apply pressure and steering, the ski will turn. If you increase edge angle, pressure, or steering, the ski turns more sharply.

Once a carved turn is begun, additional pressure is applied to the ski by the skier's mass trying to move outside of the turn arc while the carving edge provides resistance. Study photo 28 and imagine the function of centrifugal force and edge angle. Good skiers utilize these forces to control the bend in their ski. (See also photos 6, 7, and 9.)

The arc of a turn remains constant as long as the pressure, edge angle, steering input, and terrain remain constant. Any change in these factors alters the turning radius of the ski. Changes in speed or turning arc significantly affect the pressure a skier's mass exerts on a ski.

Moving the pressure distribution forward, neutral, or aft on a ski changes the arc it will carve. Pressure is distributed to a ski through a skier's boot. Press forward in the boot, and pressure is distributed more on the front of the ski. Stand neutral in the boot, and pressure will be centered on the ski. Stand on your heels, or lean back in the boot, and pressure is distributed more toward the tail. (See drawing 12.)

PRESSURE DISTRIBUTION

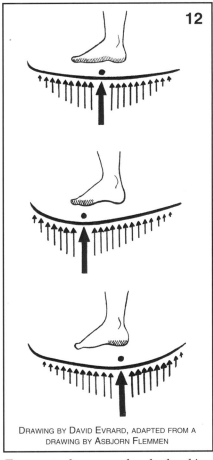

DRAWING BY DAVID EVRARD, ADAPTED FROM A DRAWING BY ASBJORN FLEMMEN

Top, neutral pressure bends the ski on an even arc. Middle, forward pressure bends the front of the ski more than the back. At bottom, aft pressure bends the back of the ski more than the front.

28

ZOOM

This is an extraordinary photo of reverse camber. Peter Roth (GER) carves a turn of such short radius that even at slalom speeds a great deal of pressure is applied to the ski.

Forward pressure distribution bends the front of a ski more than the back.
This helps to initiate turns, or to shorten the radius of turns in progress. (See photo 29.)

TEAM RUSSELL

Karen Percy pressures the front of her ski(s) to start a turn. This movement is instinctive for a skier of Karen's ability. Athletic skiers use forward pressure to initiate nearly all turns.

Neutral pressure distribution bends a ski on an even arc. This is ideal for sustained turns of a constant radius. (See photo 30.)

THOR KALLERUD

Frank Picard (FRA) stands in the middle of his ski to sustain a turn of constant radius. The front and back of his downhill ski are bent almost equally. Picard was silver medalist in DH at the 1992 Olympics.

Aft pressure distribution bends the back of a ski more than the front. This is useful at the end of quick, accelerating turns, for turns of minimal direction change, or at the end of turns where the traverse provides time to re-center your balance. (See photo 31.)

31

Thor Kallerud

Alberto Tomba (ITA) loads the tail of his ski at the end of this turn. Note that he does not have to sit in the back seat to do this. He applies pressure to the tail while keeping his body well centered over his downhill ski. Tomba has won 33 world cup races and five Olympic medals (3 gold, 2 silver). He is one of the finest alpine skiers in the history of the sport.

Now, please slow down and think carefully. All turns must begin with some shortening of the turn radius. Thus, the most efficient way to initiate turns is to use forward pressure. This helps the ski tip to lead the entire edge into a shorter radius. Nearly all turns begin with forward pressure on the ski. Turns finish with either neutral or aft pressure.

All pressure is applied to a ski through the boot. The subtlest changes in pressure are distributed through the boot sole as a skier stands more on the ball of his foot, the center, or the heel. Stronger forces are distributed by leveraging against the cuff. In all cases, the boot forms the critical suspension link between a skier's body and his skis.

One of the joys of using ski design to create turning forces is the constant opportunity a skier has to experiment and innovate. Every turn is different. Infinite combinations of edging, pressuring, and steering can be explored. Each produces a different response from the ski. Good skiers "play" constantly with their edges in the snow as one discovery follows another.

Chapter 12

Controlling the Ski

There are three things you can do to control a ski in the snow: You can **edge** it, **pressure** it, and **steer** it. All turns result from a ski's response to some combination of these forces. Expert skiers apply these forces with greater skill and variety than less accomplished skiers. To become an athletic skier, you must have a clear understanding of edging, pressuring, steering, and of their relationship to one another. (See drawing 13.)

DRAWING BY DIANE BODE

13   *To control a ski in the snow: You can edge it, pressure it, and steer it.*

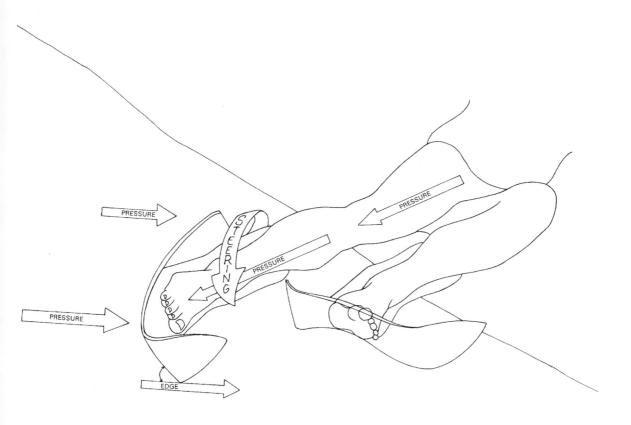

EDGE THE SKI

A ski can be edged by knee angulation, hip angulation, body lean, or any combination of these. In addition, subtle edge adjustments are continuously made with the ankle.

The quickest way to change edge angle is by knee movement. Turns made close to the fall line require little more than knee angulation to edge the skis. As it is closest to the ski, knee angulation involves the least movement of body mass, and requires the fewest associated balancing movements. Photo 32 shows Karen Percy using knee angulation to achieve the edge angle she requires at the start of a turn. Karen tucks her right knee in so her ski will be on edge when it first contacts the snow. This subtle movement of the knee is the most efficient way Karen can edge her ski and begin this turn with a pure carving action. You must edge first to begin a turn without skidding.

TEAM RUSSELL

32

Much stronger knee angulation can be used for sharper turns in slalom or whenever strong edge angles are required for quick, dynamic turns in free skiing. In photo 33, Scot Schmidt uses extreme knee angulation (combined with hip angulation) to create a strong edge angle on his left ski. We can only guess how he will use this dramatically edged ski. Will he apply forward pressure to the ski and initiate a sharp right turn? Will he use this edged ski as a platform for a lateral step? Or, is he going to let his body come straight toward the camera while his feet cross dramatically under his center of mass? The position of his left hand and the focus of his eyes tells us he is going to direct his feet quickly under his CM until his right ski is well on edge and he can carve a turn to his left. In the next second, Scott's right ski may be edged as much as his left ski is in this photo.

TEAM RUSSELL **33**

As speed increases, or the radius of a turn decreases, skiers require more inward lean to maintain balance, and greater edge angles to assist carving. For these turns, hip angulation is used, and may be combined with knee angulation. Photo 34 shows Julie Parisien (USA) using strong hip angulation in a difficult slalom turn. The edge angle seen here is extreme for slalom where speeds are modest and turns are often close to the fall line. This turn involves a major direction change at a challenging speed. Julie, who was the 1992 World Cup Slalom Champion, has the tools to master the challenge.

PENTAPHOTO

For long radius turns at high speeds, inclination of the entire body is efficient. This strong position is seen in fast giant slalom, super G, and downhill races. Minimal knee or hip angulation is used. We describe this position as the "bicycle lean angle" because the metaphor so clearly defines the action. We like our students to use angulation on skis as naturally as on a bike. (See photos 35 and 36.)

35

HIRO YAKUSHI

Kjetil-Andre Aamodt (NOR) uses full body inclination in this high speed turn. Aamodt won two silver medals and a bronze at the Lillehammer Olympics, and was the 1994 World Cup Overall Champion.

ERIK OSTLING

Alta skier, Jerry Larson, uses inclination as naturally on a bicycle as on skis. Or is it as naturally on skis as on a bicycle? Jerry wins races in both sports.

When extreme edge angles are required, knee and hip angulation are combined with inward body lean. Most recreational skiers will seldom use more than 30 degrees of edge. But strong skiers, with good carving skills, often use 45 to 60 degrees of edge. Racers use even more for sharp turns at high speed. (See photos throughout this book.)

Angulation is both a natural movement of balance, and a method of edging your skis. Good skiers do not consciously plan to create 12 or 20 or 60 degrees of angulation for a specific turn. They think of the feel their skis have in the snow. They edge and pressure their skis as necessary to make them carve on the line they choose. They edge by moving their knees, and hips, and bodies to the inside. For good skiers, these movements are as instinctive as leaning when turning a bicycle. Don't think too much about angulation. Snow skiing is not as difficult as some try to make it.

PRESSURE THE SKI.

For all carved turns, pressure is required to bend the ski into reverse camber. (See photos 9 and 28.) The sharper a turn, the more pressure is needed. Pressure is increased on a ski:

1. by standing on one ski—which doubles the weight on it compared to a two ski stance.
2. by "rising." Becoming taller exerts an equal and opposite downward force on your ski.
3. by tightening the radius of a turn so centrifugal force increases the pressure of your body against your ski.
4. by adding steering forces to an edged ski—which tightens the radius of a turn.
5. by increasing your speed (when turning).

Pressure is decreased on a ski by the opposite actions:

1. by moving your weight from one ski to two.
2. by "sinking." Becoming shorter reduces the pressure on your skis.
3. by lengthening the radius of a turn.
4. by decreasing steering forces to an edged ski.
5. by decreasing your speed (when turning).

All of these movements can be combined in infinite variations. Athletic skiers are fluid and dynamic. There's no "correct way" to change the pressure on your skis. For even the simplest wedge turn, movement is dynamic. Speed, edge angle, turn radius, terrain, and body position are always in flux. If you're self conscious, or you think too much about these movements, your skiing becomes forced and static.

You must be *foot aware*, and always processing feedback from your skis. Whatever your skis are doing in the snow is a result of the amount of edge, pressure, and steering you apply to them, and the timing of the pressure cycles you use. To ski well, you must be skilled in the use of pressure.

We don't teach a "specific turn" to skiers. It's more useful to help them understand how edge, pressure, and steering affect their skis—then encourage exploration. We give skiers tools for learning, and tell them to "go play." Experience is the best teacher.

To understand this, consider a metaphor: How do you teach people to use the brake when they learn to drive a car? Do you tell them how to retract their leg, move it 4 inches to the left, extend it to the brake pedal, and apply 10 pounds of pressure? Or do you explain how the brake works, make certain they have room to err, and let them experiment? The latter method works best. In the same way, we teach how edging works, and let skiers experiment. Then teach how pressure works, and let them experiment some more. This teaching is best done at slow speeds and on terrain where there is room to err.

The best skiers adjust pressure forward and back on their skis by moving their feet. It's quicker to move your feet forward or back than to move your body. You can experiment with this idea while standing in a lift line. Stand with your weight slightly on the balls of your feet, and press lightly against the tongue of your boot. Then push your feet 4–6 inches ahead. The pressure moves quickly to the middle of your skis, or even a little aft. Next, start in the same slightly forward position and (without sliding your feet forward) move your body back. This movement is slow, and uses the big muscles in your torso. This is not efficient. Good skiers adjust fore and aft pressure by moving their feet, not their bodies.

STEER THE SKI

Any action that applies a twisting force to the ski is a form of steering. Steering can be one subtle movement, or the combination of many active ones. We think of steering as a broad spectrum of muscular activity. At one end of the spectrum is the subtlest muscular guidance of a carving ski. At the other end is a pure pivot of a flat ski. In between are all forms of steering control.

In athletic skiing the use of steering *complements* the use of edge and pressure. Steering an edged ski is a direct form of pressure control. *When steering helps tighten the radius of a turn, pressure increases.* A little steering can help a ski to carve. Too much steering forces a ski to skid.

If you look again at drawing 13 on page 74, you can visualize the effects of steering on an edged ski. ***The steering force is always on the same plane as the ski base.*** When the ski is tilted on edge, the steering turns the tip of the ski down into the snow. This helps the ski to carve.

Traditionally, people think of steering as a rotational force that works on the plane of the snow surface. This is correct only for a flat ski. The more a ski is edged, the more the steering force drives the shovel of the ski into the snow. When a ski is just 10 or 15 degrees on edge, *and is carving not skidding*, controlled steering forces do not create a skid. They help to pressure the front of the ski.

Though carving skills are the foundation of athletic skiing, we are not so foolish as to think that all turns can or should be "purely carved." Turns of short radius, and turns made at slower speeds, are difficult or impossible to "pure carve." We create some turns with 99 percent edge and pressure, and 1 percent steering. Other turns are made with 10 percent edge and pressure, and 90 percent steering. The possibilities are infinite. When the use of edge and pressure are the primary forces that turn our skis, we say we are "skiing with carving skills." When steering forces are dominant, we are "skiing with skidding skills."

In athletic skiing, steering forces *supplement* the use of edge and pressure to control a ski. Edge and pressure are primary. Steering forces are secondary.

PART 4

LEARNING
CARVING SKILLS

S ince the publication of *How the Racers Ski* in 1972, there has been a continuing debate in skiing circles about how much carving should be taught in ski schools; and how important carving is for "recreational skiers." Among racers, there is no debate. Carving skills are as necessary as sticky tires on a race car. Among the best athletic skiers, there's no debate. They know what kind of skiing is the most fun to do. Among ski and boot manufacturers, there's no debate. They design their equipment to excel in the carving mode. And with the authors of this book, there's no debate. Carving is more dynamic, more athletic, and more precise.

To ski without carving skills is like playing football on wet grass without cleats. Balance is tentative. Direction changes are slow. Quick or accelerating movements are impossible. When our feet are sliding (whether on snow or on grass) our athleticism is restricted. *Learning to carve is like putting on cleats*. A carving ski provides the platform necessary for athletic movement.

Carving skills are the keys to athletic skiing. At *all* levels of instruction, our goal is clear: to help students strengthen carving elements in their skiing and reduce skidding elements. In the language of the last chapter—we help our students to expand their use of edge and pressure, and diminish their use of steering.

You can't progress in a day from mostly skidding to perfect carving. But, one day at a time, new skills can be learned. We need to define our goals, then find a way to reach them.

Chapter 13

SETTING GOALS: "SCORING TOUCHDOWNS"

A pure carved turn is one in which the tip of the ski leads the turn, and the entire ski edge passes through the same groove in the snow. There is no skidding. For many turns and many kinds of skiing, leaving tracks as in photo 37, is our goal.

THOR KALLERUD

37

Photo 37 is taken from the same action sequence as photo 3. Our interest here is not the one carved turn that Tim Hanson is making, but all the turn tracks that can be seen in the background. This hill was groomed for race training. While the coaches were setting the course, the athletes took a few warm-up runs. Skiing from arc to arc, they left as fine a collection of carved turn tracks as we have ever seen on one slope. Looking at these tracks, can you imagine the precision and fluid motion that are combined in the athletes' skiing?

Good skiers—even the best racers—don't make only carved turns and narrow tracks. Carving skills are dominant in their skiing; but they skid too—sometimes by choice, to control speed; other times by necessity, when turns are too sharp or speed is too slow for carving. In many turns, carving and skidding elements are combined. (See photo 38.)

38

ERIK OSTLING

These tracks show where carving and skidding elements have been combined. The "brush marks" are of medium width in the belly of the turns; but they narrow to a fine carving track in the transition area between the turns. These turns are made with edge, pressure and subtle steering. Ski design, not rotation, is used to create the turns. Because the terrain is almost flat, and the speeds are slow, pure carving would be difficult.

Unfortunately, many people in skiing have failed to differentiate between "a pure carved turn" and "the use of carving skills." Finding it difficult to make a perfect carved turn, they have forsaken the simpler goal of improving carving skills. A broader understanding of "carving skills" is needed, and also an understanding of why they are important.

An extended metaphor provides a framework for understanding:

THE PLAYING FIELD OF SKIING

Think of skiing as a sport done on a football field. There's an end zone and a goal line at both ends.

In the left end zone, beginners are making skidded turns on relatively flat skis. The use of steering forces is dominant, and their use of edge and pressure is minimal.

In the right end zone, athletic skiers and racers are carving turns. Their use of edge and pressure is dominant. Steering forces are supplemental.

In the middle are skiers combining elements of skidding and carving. As you move across the field from left to right, carving skills become more dominant. (See drawing 14.)

One can play (or ski) anywhere on this field, using any combination of steering and carving skills. If given a choice, however, we prefer to play at the right end of the field, where the most athletic skiers are. ***Our goal as ski teachers—and in writing this book—is to help people get to the right end zone as quickly as possible.***

Most skiers are taught skidding skills as beginners. (They start in the left end zone.) Then they are never given enough carving skills to move their skiing to the right of mid-field. Most American ski schools teach "Center-Line" now. This is a mix of skidding and carving skills somewhere between the 40-yard lines. Ski Schools that choose to play in the middle of the field don't set high enough goals for their students.

We honor all skiers on the playing field. If some are happy to play at mid-field, that's fine. But we think the further to the right you play, the more fun you can have. Athletic skiers should set high goals. If you play on a football field, you should score some touchdowns!

When athletic skiers have finished play, they leave tracks behind them as in photo 37.

14

DRAWING BY VIKI FLECKENSTEIN WOODWORTH

THE PLAYING FIELD OF SKIING

Chapter 14

LEARN TO FEEL THE SKI

If we are teaching beginners, we focus from the first lesson on foot-feel. We teach an awareness of how their skis respond to edge and pressure, and how they work in the snow. We have students *study the tracks their skis leave in the snow* — from their first wedge turn to whatever level they reach.

When teaching carving skills to intermediate or expert skiers, we ask them to ski a section of trail in any way they choose. We give no specific instruction or technical goal. When they stop, we ask what they were ***thinking*** about while skiing. Most students respond with a description of body positions or body movements.

We ask them to clear all such thoughts from their minds, and to focus their consciousness on ***feeling through the soles of their feet.*** While standing on the trail, we say, "shift your weight subtly forward and back. Feel the pressure change on the sole of your foot. Roll your skis from edge to edge, thinking only of the feedback you get through your foot. Where do you feel the pressure? Can you sense the edge of your ski in the snow? . . . Now, with this focus, let's go skiing."

With their minds clear of all thoughts but foot-awareness, our students ski with greater relaxation and more natural body positions. They have shifted from body consciousness to foot consciousness. This is a critical step for mastering carving skills and becoming expert skiers.

Modern skis are wonderful tools. They are brilliantly engineered, responsive, and energetic. When you ski, you must be aware of these tools and of how they work. ***You must think of skiing as an activity that begins in the snow, reacts through your skis, and is understood through the soles of your feet.*** Your skis, connected to your senses, must become extensions of your body, not attachments to it.

For the rest of this book, you must have this focus as you read. For every exercise or movement we describe, ***be aware of how it will feel through the soles of your feet.***

Chapter 15

WEDGE TURNS

When teaching beginners, we introduce carving skills with the first wedge turns. We explain that if they edge and pressure a ski, by standing on it in the right way, the ski will turn. Some "foot steering" is helpful; but no upper-body rotation is needed. We focus their attention on skiing with the soles of their feet. We say, "with your skis in a wedge, make ripples on the snow." This helps them to feel, and to see, how the ski edge works. As we build perceptual bridges to the foot and the ski, we eliminate rotation of the body and arms.

Humans are instinctively eye/hand coordinated. It's natural for them to "steer" or turn their bodies with hand and shoulder movements. Skiers must suppress these instincts; and replace them with eye/foot and mind/foot coordination skills. *A ski is a tool that we "hold" with our feet, and use with our feet.* It makes no more sense to swing a ski with our arms than to swing a hammer with our legs.

In athletic skiing, the upper body remains quiet and stable. We ski with our feet, our ankles, and our knees. When teaching carving skills to advanced skiers, and even to racers, we use wedge turns to teach these fundamentals. (See photo 39, next page.)

In high speed skiing, many movements are blended so quickly together that it's difficult for the "minds eye" to separate them. But wedge turns, done at walking speed, can be seen like slow motion movies: Each input of the skier, and the response it generates from the ski, can be understood separately. We develop understanding at slow speed; then perform at high speed.

What can we learn from wedge turns?

We can explore all the different ways our skis react to edge, pressure, and steering. We can experiment with different amounts of edge—10, 20, or 30 degrees. We can explore the reaction of our skis to forward, neutral, and aft pressure. We can play with different amounts of pressure, using different rhythms of weighting and unweighting. We can experience how tightening a turn adds pressure to our skis.

All these movements are done in turns that combine carving and skidding elements. No wedge turn can be a pure carved turn. But we can skid more or skid less. We can use edge and pressure to help turn our skis from the front; or we can push on our tails and skid. We can experiment until we get our skis to turn "by just standing on them in the right way."

We can change the shape of our turns—making some with a constant radius, others with a changing radius. In all of these explorations, we learn to use edge, pressure, and steering to control our skis. No upper body rotation is required. (We shoot students who use rotation in wedge turns.)

In slow speed wedge turns, we explore all the fundamentals of carving. We learn the language and feel of athletic skiing.

39

ERIK OSTLING

Wedge turns are made with the same skills as high speed racing turns: edge the ski; apply pressure in the right way; steer a little if necessary; and let the skis create the turn. Warren teaches carving skills by doing wedge turns because they're like slow motion movies. As the speed of athletic movement is reduced, the smallest details are more easily seen and understood. Warren's upper body is quiet and stable in this turn. He adjusts edge and pressure with subtle movements of his left knee and ankle — then just stands on the ski and lets it do the work it is designed to do.

Before moving on from wedge turns, we demonstrate the difference between the use of primarily carving elements and primarily skidding ones. We ask our students to make a long series of wedge turns on a consistent slope. First, they must use carving elements for four turns—maintaining the wedge, but making every effort to control their skis with edge and pressure. Then they skid four turns—pushing their heels out and letting their skis act as a brake. Carve four, skid four, etc., etc. The changes in speed, and in resistance of the ski against the snow, are surprising. In the same radius turns, the skidded turns slow you to half the speed you generate when using more carving skills.

This simple exercise demonstrates perfectly the difference between playing to the left or right of mid-field. When skidding elements are dominant, your skis act as a brake, and are always resisting the mountain. When carving elements are dominant, your skis work in harmony with the mountain by letting the snow shape them and help them to turn. When carving, you experience the gliding potential of your skis. You learn to "let the skis run" and to seek speed from your skis.

At this point, both skiers and readers may say: "Wait a minute. If I don't use my skis for a brake, how do I control my speed?" In answering this question, we teach one of the most important lessons in athletic skiing. ***You control speed by selection of line.*** To go slower, turn farther from the fall line, or turn more across the hill. To go faster, ski closer to the fall line. At all levels of skiing, we control speed in this manner.

When free skiing, racers say: "Pick a slow line and go fast on it." In this way they control their speed; they learn to let their skis glide; they master carving skills; and they ski in harmony with the mountain.

We can learn all of these skills doing wedge turns with edge lock.

Chapter 16

Wedge Turns with Edge Lock

This is the first of two exercises we use to teach the feeling of riding a ski on a perfectly clean edge, with no skidding at all. Select a wide, gentle slope that is smoothly groomed. Make a series of wedge turns connected by long traverses. Though there will be skidding in the turns, **there must be no skidding or sliding in each traverse.** Your goal is to ride a clean, carving edge, and to leave a track no wider than your ski. (See photo 40.)

Maintain your speed between a fast walk and a slow jog. *To control your speed, turn as far past the fall line as necessary.* In this exercise, as in advanced free skiing, do *not* control your speed by using the ski as a brake. Use line and terrain to control speed. Let your skis run as fast as they will go. In these slow speed maneuvers, you can learn to seek speed from your skis—to use them as accelerators not brakes. We pick a slow line and go as fast as possible on it.

At the end of each traverse, make a strong wedge turn to a new direction. Let ski design, not rotation, turn your outside ski. Roll your knee in to provide edge angle. Then just stand on the ski, pressing it into reverse camber. A little forward pressure helps the tip to lead the turn. If you apply the right edge and pressure to the ski, it will turn without further effort on your part.

At the end of each turn—in the instant your downhill ski is pointing in the direction you wish it to go—"lock" the ski on edge. To achieve "edge lock," pressure the middle of your ski and subtly increase edge angle. It will take some practice and concentration on your task to achieve edge lock in the instant your ski is pointing on the line you wish to traverse. The tendency of most skiers is to skid for a while, then straighten out on a carving ski. One of the goals we are working for in high speed skiing is to achieve edge lock as early as possible in turns that begin with some skidding. Learn here at slow speed. Perform, later, at high speed.

Make long traverses between each turn until you feel really comfortable on a non-skidding ski. **Feel the whole ski edge run in the same groove. Feel the stability of the platform and the sense of gliding.** Throughout each traverse, maintain your stance at wedge turn width—just flatten your uphill ski so it provides minimum resistance. Look again at photo 40.

40

Look carefully at the track made by Warren's left ski. At the end of the wedge turn (seen at the back of the photo), Warren "locks" the ski immediately on edge. He makes the transition from the skidded wedge turn to the carving traverse at the earliest possible moment. With this exercise, Warren teaches the feeling of riding a pure-carving edge though he is skiing at walking speed.

When you are comfortable and skilled at non-skidding traverses, experiment with extra edge angle. Be goofy. This should be fun. Edge your ski 60 or 70 degrees. Can you touch your knee to the snow? (See photos 41 and 42.)

ERIK OSTLING

Warren does "goofy edge-locks"; but the learning is serious. With this fun exercise, he introduces skiers to the extreme range of motion they can later achieve in athletic skiing. Students learn what it feels like to have their supporting ski more than 60 degrees on edge. They experience positions of extreme angulation. At slow speeds, they begin to feel the body positions and ski responses they will later experiment with at high speed.

Warren's exploration of extreme edging movements isn't necessary for slow speed turns; but the end goal we're seeking is to master extreme edging and carving skills. At 5 mph, you can explore skills and feelings you will later use at higher speeds.

Photo 42 shows Matt Grosjean (USA) combining edge lock with extreme angulation in a World Cup slalom race. Matt has complete trust in the carving edge of his right ski. Edge lock exercises help less accomplished skiers to develop this trust and improve their carving skills.

ZOOM

Chapter 17

RAILROAD TRACK TURNS

We have travelled many hundreds of miles doing wide stance, pure carve, parallel turns—with our feet 24-36 inches apart. (Some instructors call these "Gliding Edge-Lock".) Because of the tracks they leave in the snow, we think of them as "Railroad Track Turns" (RR for short). We do them, whether teaching or free skiing, wherever there's easy terrain or a flat section in a trail. Cat walks are great! (See photo 43.)

43

ERIK OSTLING

We learn three things from Railroad Track Turns:

First, we learn to begin turns without skidding, which is the hardest skill in carving.

Second, we learn to ride a pure carving edge through the belly of a turn, which is the most joyful part of carving.

Third, we learn to explore how a carving ski responds to various amounts of edge and pressure.

These tracks were made doing "Railroad Track Turns." Can you duplicate these — leaving no signs of skidding at any point in your turns?

Railroad track turns offer the easiest way to experience the pure carving action of a ski. There is no way to "teach" carving that is as successful as experiencing it. ***You can't sneak up on carving skills***—trying to gradually make transitions from more skidding to less skidding to no skidding. Most ski schools fail to teach carving effectively because they use the "sneak up on it" method. RR Turns immerse you in pure carving. Your feet feel. Your muscles get programmed. Your mind understands. ***You succeed at carving in the first few minutes you make RR turns.*** You learn the skill on easy terrain, then work to apply it on steeper slopes. (See photo 44, next page.)

This double image photo shows the RR turn exercise in the larger image; and dynamic, parallel skiing in the smaller image. In both photos, the right or outside leg is in a similar position. Warren just stands on his right ski, pressing it into reverse camber, and goes along for the ride. The movement, in both turns, is exhilarating and free.

The magic of RR turns is that they put you so effortlessly on an edged and tracking ski. *They allow you to feel a turn begin without skidding.* This is the hardest part of carving to learn. The challenge is to get the ski on edge without pushing it or sliding it to the side. In advanced parallel skiing, this requires "cross-under" skills (divergence of ski line and body line) with a high degree of trust that after weight transfer, the new ski which is on edge and outside your body, will support you. (See photo 45.)

This is an important concept in athletic skiing. A study of the dynamic photos throughout this book shows skiers ***trusting*** their skis to support them when the skis are far out from under their bodies. You cannot trust a skidding ski in this position. You can trust a carving ski. As carving skills are learned, trust grows. It is important to have this trust at the start of all turns.

RR turns teach us to carve at the start of our turns, and to trust an edged ski. Look again at the large image in photo 44, and look ahead to drawing 15 on page 101. The basic stance in which RR turns are done puts both skis on their inside edge. Because your feet are wider than your hips, angulation is "pre-set" on both legs. You can turn on either ski by simply weighting or pressuring it, and bending it into reverse camber. As the ski is on edge when the pressure is applied, it will begin carving.

The more you experience this feeling, the more comfortable you become with your ski on edge, and away from your body. ***With sufficient repetition, you can program your muscle memory to edge a ski before you pressure it.***

LEARNING RR TURNS

Select nearly flat terrain where you can "schuss" straight ahead between jogging and running speed. Be sure there's a good run out so you have no worries about excessive speed. (You'll be surprised how fast you can go on a gentle slope.) Place your feet 2–3 feet apart. Be certain that your skis are parallel and that both skis are tilted onto their inside edge. You must stand in an "A frame"—with your knees closer together than your feet.

45

Werner Perathoner (ITA) shows complete trust in the carving edge of his right ski though it is far out from under his body. This trust is evident in the most dynamic photos throughout this book.

In both photo images, Warren's body position, angulation, and stance on his right ski are nearly identical. So is the action of his ski in the snow. It's easiest to turn without skidding in the RR turn stance; but after mastering the skill in RR turns, it is easily applied to high speed, parallel skiing.

Start straight down the fall line with your weight distributed evenly on both skis. From this position, shift your weight first to your right ski for a few seconds. Then to your left ski. Go back and forth. *Do not push your skis away from your body. Do not push your skis into a stem or even 1 degree of a wedge. For these turns, no steering is required.* Only edge and pressure. **When you weight a ski, just stand on it. Don't push it or twist it.** Keep your skis as parallel as you can, and leave tracks in the snow as in photo 43. When you weight one ski, leave the other in light contact with the snow.

To better understand these concepts as you read, stand wherever you are and imagine you are skiing. Go through the movements described in the paragraph above. Feel the angulated position you have over each foot. Imagine how your skis will respond to pressure. Can you shift your weight from one foot to the other **without pushing on your heels?**

Nearly all skiers, when they first try RR turns, push outward on their tails. This is an ingrained habit developed over all the years they have skied. The muscle patterns are well established. You must concentrate and discipline yourself to break this habit. (See drawing 15.)

The other habit you must work hard to break is that of trying to change the direction of your skis too quickly. For carving, you must be *patient* at the start of a turn. To understand, think of driving a car. Good drivers don't jerk the wheel at the start of a turn; they ease into a turn, moving the wheel progressively. Skiers who skid, "jerk the wheel" at the start of turns—swinging their skis quickly through many degrees of arc. RR turns help you to learn patience, and to trust your skis. Photos 50 and 51 (pages 118 and 119) demonstrate patience and edging a ski before turning it.

Hint: Don't try to turn more than a few degrees out of the fall line. Most people try to turn 15–20 degrees, and lacking patience for such a direction change, they must push their tails out. When learning RR turns, it's *very important* to select proper terrain so you have no need for braking or speed control. You must let your skis run. You are seeking all possible speed—using all the acceleration gravity provides, and dissipating as little energy as possible. You are discovering skiing without skidding. We want you to learn this with total relaxation and no fear of speed.

After you get RR turns working well (leaving tracks that are purely carved), you can proceed to a number of interesting games. Here are a dozen variations of the basic RR turn. Each one produces a different reaction from your skis.

1. Change the edge angle you use:
   a. by taking a wider or narrower stance.
   b. by moving your knees further in or out.

2. Change the pressure you apply to each ski:
   a. by shifting a different % of your weight to each ski.
   b. by different rhythms of unweighting—changing your up and down pressure

RR turns require edge first, then pressure. Steering is minimal. Note the fluid, continuous line that joins one turn to the next. The skis are never pushed sideways. There is no skidding. The entire ski edge runs in the same groove in the snow. In RR turns, you experience the pure carving action of a ski.

cycles.

   3. Change the pressure distribution along your ski:
     a. by pressing on the ball of your foot and the tongue of your boot.
     b. by distributing your weight evenly along your foot sole.
     c. by pressing on your heel and the back of your boot shaft.

What different reactions do you get from your skis when applying pressure more forward, neutral, or aft? The ski turns sharpest when the tip is most weighted, and least sharp as the tail is weighted. The speed is greatest on the tail.

   4. Change the length of time you stand on each ski:
     a. in quick turns, stand for one or two seconds on each ski.
     b. in medium turns, stand for three to five seconds on each edge.
     c. in long turns, stand for six or more seconds on each edge. Ride the edge in long, graceful arcs—just standing on the ski and flowing with it.

   5. Change the speed at which you ski:
     a. by choosing steeper or flatter terrain.
     b. by turning more or less out of the fall line. You will find that speed changes only slightly whether you turn 2 degrees or 10. A ten degree turn provides little resistance on a carving ski. By contrast, if skidding turns, each additional degree of arc provides significantly more braking.

Twelve variations are listed above. In various combinations, these provide more than a hundred different ways to explore how edge and pressure affect a ski. Think about this! Here are 100+ ways to explore skiing in one basic stance, on almost flat terrain. *If you are curious and creative, you can learn more about skiing from these exercises than from any other lessons we can give.* You can discover the fascination of playing with your skis. You can return to these exercises any number of times and always learn more from them. After twenty years, we still find these games interesting and challenging.

Throughout these exercises, remember to stay focused on snow, ski, boot, and foot feel. If you are thoughtful, you can apply this knowledge to all your skiing. To learn carving, the RR turn is the best teaching tool we know.

One of the great joys of carving is learning to feel your skis accelerate. Racers work constantly to achieve maximum acceleration in their skiing. Their credo for free skiing is: "Pick a slow line and go fast on it." This forces them to exploit gravity, and eliminate drag. Skidders choose a fast line and go slow on it. They resist gravity, and create drag. YUK! This is painful to think about, and more painful to do. Our advice to all skiers is: "Brake when you need to. Accelerate when you can."

When you master carving, *you can flow down a mountain rather than skid against it.* An instructor we canted correctly, and taught carving skills to for a day, said this to us: "In twenty years of skiing, I have never felt so free on a mountain. I could extend and trust my edge. I have skied faster and with more freedom than ever before. ***This is so much fun!***" What we did for this woman was teach her to ski without one foot "riding the brake."

When doing RR turns, you can experience the smallest changes of speed with surprising sensitivity. A gliding or carving ski, because it has less vibration, provides more precise feedback than a skidding ski. Thus, as we learn carving skills, we become increasingly sensitive to the subtlest changes in acceleration.

When learning carving skills, it isn't necessary to do only RR turns for a day or a week. Go skiing. Have fun. Pick a trail with some flat sections in it and a run out at the bottom. Each time you come to terrain that's flat enough to schuss, practice RR turns. Do them all over the mountain (wherever the terrain is appropriate). Play first with subtle variations of edge and pressure; then experiment with all the edge angle you can get, and as much pressure as you can generate. What ski responses can you discover? Can you begin to duplicate these in "normal" parallel skiing?

Three thoughts are important before we move to other exercises.

First, in all your skiing, be aware of the tracks you leave in the snow. If you ski under a lift, leave tracks where you can find them on the ride up. Study other tracks from the lift. Watch other skiers and look at the tracks they are making. You'll learn that the most exciting skiers leave the narrowest tracks. Look again at photos 3 and 37 which show the playing field after the racers have left.

Second, we'd like to stress that doing the exercises listed here, and working on carving skills, should always be approached as "play." It's fun to explore for new responses from your skis. Wherever the terrain is appropriate, use RR turns to add variety and exploration to your skiing.

Third, you must understand that pure carved turns (which RR turns are) have a fairly long radius. You can't ski this way on steep or bumpy terrain (unless you are very good); *but for all turns on all terrain, you can expand carving elements, and decrease skidding elements.* The skills and feelings you learn in the exercises given here can be applied to some degree in all turns. You are learning to edge and pressure a ski to control its turning arc, rather than to skid and push it. When you understand these principles, *and have felt them in your skiing,* then you have acquired the tools to continue learning. You are moving closer to the right end zone. Continued progress depends on your natural athleticism, your commitment to keep exploring, and your time on snow.

In the next chapter, we'll give you some exercises that help to develop carving skills.

Chapter 18

CARVING AND EDGING EXERCISES

Many exercises are particularly useful for developing carving skills. These five are our favorites:

1. **Skating**. On flat, or almost flat terrain, all forms of skating exercises are good for your skiing. A skating step can only be made from a carving edge. Skating steps require good balance in the middle of your ski, efficient weight transfers, and independent leg action.

   One of the best early season exercises for skiing is to skate on a flat, snow-covered field. When coaching racers, we take them to a football or soccer field when the first snowfall covers the grass. On slalom skis, ten laps around the goal posts provide a good workout. Skating on flat ground strengthens all the right leg muscles, and gets the racers working for speed and gliding on their edges. Slalom courses can be set. Games of "Rover Come Over" test speed and agility. All skating workouts require excellent balance and being well centered on your skis.

   Other kinds of skating are good too. Ice skates, in-line skates, and cross-country skiing all offer perfect opportunities to glide without skidding. Ice skating is wonderful training for alpine skiing. On ice skates, you skid only to slow down or to stop. At all other times you carve and use your edges to provide a platform for turning, accelerating, and lateral movements. The muscle patterns are similar to snow skiing.

2. **"One Thousand Steps."** These are pure carve movements. To control speed, they are best done on relatively flat terrain. They are small, divergent steps made from a non-skidding edge. They leave tracks in the snow as in drawing 16.

   "One Thousand Steps" stimulate good balance and adjusting forward and back as you move from one foot to another. Be quick and light on your feet. On both your uphill and downhill ski—the inside edge of one ski and the outside edge of the other—you move continually from carving edge to carving edge. In quick succession, you establish a platform on one ski and then on the other. The experience of stepping onto a clearly edged ski is good training for a variety of movements that are basic to athletic skiing.

ONE THOUSAND STEPS

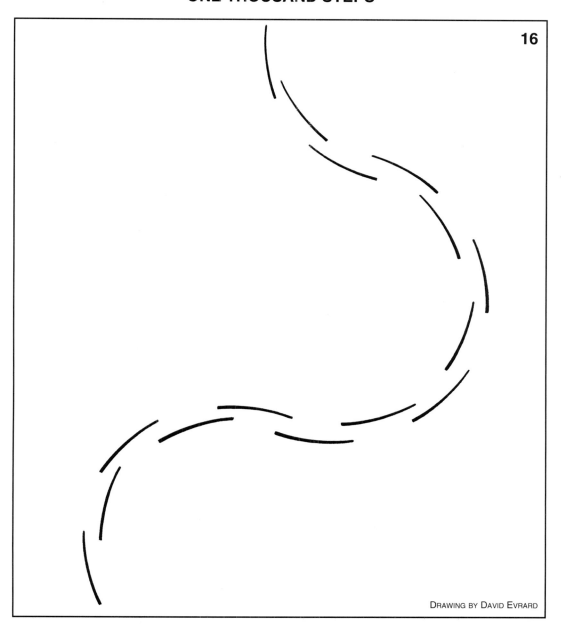

The 1000 steps exercise leaves tracks like those shown here.

46

3. **Diminishing Wedge to Parallel.** On gentle terrain, *at slow speed*, start down the fall line in a wedge position. Shift all your weight to your right ski with immediate edge lock. Ride this ski edge for a few seconds, then shift to your left ski, also with edge lock. Do not skid. Shift back and forth from one ski to the other. As your speed increases, let the angle of your wedge diminish, and your feet come closer and closer together until doing clean, nearly pure carved turns. This exercise improves edging skills, agility, and good weight transfer from ski to ski.

4. **Hop Turns or Zottos.** These are powerful edge control and carving exercises. You never stay long enough on an edged ski to have a sense of gliding. You must, however, have powerful edging skills and perfectly centered balance. (See photo 46.) On slopes ranging anywhere from flat to moderately steep, go as slowly as possible down the fall line—springing off the snow, turning your skis in the air, landing on a non-skidding edge, and rebounding immediately into the next turn. (You can do four turns in the time it takes to read that sentence.) On a gentle slope, this exercise is a technical challenge. As the slope steepens, the demands become more physical and more athletic. Try them on a variety of slopes. Don't be discouraged if you find them difficult. You're an athletic skier, and need to be challenged. As your carving and edging skills improve, hop turns get easier. Do fifty a day. They develop power and agility as well as edging skills.

David Evrard does hop turns. If you look at the tracks behind him, you can see he has made a long series of turns with great precision. Each edge set is clean and sharp. There is no sign of skidding. Dave rebounds instantly from one turn to the next. His stance is upright, and he is perfectly centered over his skis.

5. "Snake Turns." These are a series of *pure* carved turns done on one ski. They require precise alignment, balance in the center of your ski, and subtle edging skills. You must have equal control on both the inside and outside edges of your ski. (See photos 47 and 48.)

ERIK OSTLING

47

Snake turns require that you stand in exactly the right way on your ski—providing just enough edge angle and pressure to coax the ski into subtle changes of direction. There is no weighting or unweighting. Pressure remains constant on the ski. Your weight on one ski provides all the reverse camber you need. There is no clear delineation between left and right turns. The path of the ski is a flowing movement. Snake turns offer a nice complement to hop turns. The hop turn is quick and explosive. The snake turn is soft and flowing. Together, these exercises cover the full range of movement from hard edge set to no edge set at all. In snake turns, you change edges and direction as smoothly as water flows through a hose. The fluid movement is delightful, and exemplifies one of the best aspects of carving turns.

Snake turns develop skills for changing edges and direction without steering, skidding, rotation, or lateral push of your skis. If you can do snake turns, you can initiate turns without skidding. In many free-skiing and racing turns, we step onto the outside edge of our uphill ski, then change edges in a subtle, flowing motion. The part of this turn just before and after the edge change is similar to a snake turn. The challenge is to change edges and direction without skidding your tails. This is not easy, but its lots of fun when you master it. Perfect canting (i.e., lateral balance) is a prerequisite for doing snake turns.

Each of the exercises in the last five chapters, helps you to build the skills, the feelings, and the understandings that lead to advanced parallel skiing at the carving end of our playing field.

None of these exercises should be viewed as an end in itself. All are stepping stones and learning tools. They're fun to do, and a challenge to do well. They are games we play in the larger process of learning about skiing. There are countless other games and exercises we do with specific students on specific terrain. There is no "right way" to teach skiing skills. We are less interested in your mastering a given exercise than in your learning from it some skills that will help you to learn by yourself after you leave our class.

In this "snake turn", David is seen carving on his outside edge. Look at the track his ski has left. The snow here is warm and unstable so it rolls out of the groove even when the turn is perfectly carved. The subtlest adjustments of edge and pressure are required to lure the ski into these gentle, carving arcs.

48

Erik Ostling

"There is no clear delineation between one turn and another. The path of the ski is a flowing movement."

Please note that we have never mentioned a "perfect body position" for any of the above exercises. We have focused on the *result* of all movements—looking at the tracks left in the snow, achieving solid edge platforms, and finding good balance. We have never been self-conscious about "proper form" or "how we look." If a skier's suspension system is well aligned, we know that form will follow function. We have been less structured than most ski school classes. We have put the responsibility for learning on our students' abilities to explore and discover.

All of our exercises have helped us to understand the use of our skis to create turning forces. If you have learned enough, you are ready for advanced parallel skiing. Carving will be our method. Athletic skiing, with freedom and spontaneity, is our goal.

Before moving on to Part 5, we suggest you return briefly to Chapter 2 and review the traits of an Athletic Skier. These should have broader meanings for you now than when you began reading. As we approach advanced parallel skiing, it will help to have these images in mind. The pictures will be especially helpful. Pictures are better teachers than words. Keep these images of "really good skiing" in mind as you take your next steps toward the right end of our playing field.

Kerrin Lee-Gartner (CAN)

"You must master the art of carving, trust your instincts, and learn to use your skis like cleats."

PART 5

SKI FAST AND
LEAVE NARROW TRACKS

As we approach the most dynamic elements of skiing, the language of technique and ski mechanics begins to fail, and a new language of image and instinct becomes more helpful. We must begin to learn by imagination, feeling, and exploration—not by steps A, B, C. We must begin to think as athletes and to learn from other sports.

Let's begin with an image: Stand with us on a rounded knoll watching the young girls from Burke Mountain Academy training Giant Slalom. Each racer has a different stance and posture, a unique signature for her skiing. One team, one coach, but many styles. These girls are going 40 miles an hour and carving turns on ice that are hard to believe. Then Marie-Michelle comes by—faster than any other—and makes a lateral move on the knoll that leaves us gasping.

"Did you see that?" we ask in unison, shaking our heads in disbelief. M&M has made a turn that defies description. With stop-frame-photos and a hundred pages of text, we could not explain the magic we have seen. Looking back, eight months later, this one turn stands in our memory as a symbol for athletic skiing. It defines a standard all skiers can aspire to. This single turn captured our imagination and helped us define an athletic skier.

If we asked M&M, "How did you do that?" she would smile, shrug her shoulders, and laugh. She hasn't a clue. *She just did it.* On her skis, at 40+ miles an hour, she made a phenomenally athletic movement with no more conscious thought than she would give to side-stepping a puddle in the road. She was at point A. She wanted to be at point B. So she went there. Her movement on skis was as natural as Michael Jordan's cutting for the basket, or O.J. Simpson's lateral move to slip a tackle.

Can Michael or O.J. tell you how they do it? No. They move by instinct. Jordan has sticky soles on his Nikes. Simpson had cleats on his. And M&M has sharp edges on her skis. All three act and react to the opportunities in front of them. ***The challenge for skiers is to move as easily on skis as in sneakers.*** M&M and thousands of other young racers have learned that. The goal, to a significant degree, is attainable for the readers of this book. To reach this goal, you must master the art of carving, trust your instincts, and learn to use your skis like cleats.

When *How the Racers Ski* was published in 1972, it was clear that the technique of the best racers provided a logical and attainable goal for recreational skiers. The racers were striving for "optimum balance, economy of motion, and use of their skis to create turning forces." These goals have provided a continuing standard for modern ski technique for the past twenty years.

As we began work on this book, and spent time watching World Cup and junior races, we first thought race technique was diverging markedly from "normal skiing." The racers were so athletic we wondered if the public should even try to ski the same way. We were prepared to say that race technique, like Formula 1 cars, was becoming too sophisticated to be copied by recreational skiers. After a winter of immersion in all levels of skiing, we no longer think so. We are again confident that racers are leading our sport in a direction we should all be going.

The racers of the 90's exhibit the same fundamentals they did twenty years ago. With help from superior skis and boots, they have added a delightful new element to skiing. ***This new element is dynamic, athletic movement.*** Torjus Berge shows it on the cover. Stephanie Schuster shows it in photo 2, and other racers show it throughout the book. They are more dynamic and more athletic than most recreational skiers can hope to be. These racers are superior athletes. They are exceptionally strong, and they train for competition. But they are *not* doing things that normal people cannot do. *They are simply doing them at a higher level.* We respect that level, and copy what we can. Good racers are more fully exploiting the skis now available. ***We should be inspired by their achievements, set higher goals for ourselves, and learn to better use our skis.***

If you ask World Cup coaches what they are working on, or what the secrets of the best racers are, the answers are always the same: ***"Fundamentals" and "Balance."*** They repeat these words over and over in conversations on technique. What fundamentals? ***"Carving skills—especially at the top of the turn."*** They are working at starting turns without skidding. They say: ***"To win, you must carve where others are skidding. Everyone carves on the flats and the medium pitches. When you carve on the steeps, then you can win."***

The best racers are working to become more skilled at "edge first, then pressure." They are working on pressure skills, trying to find the most efficient ways to use their skis. They are working at running their center of mass on the shortest possible line, and their skis on divergent lines that allow the best carving and the least skidding.

In short, *the best racers in the world are working on the same fundamentals we are teaching at every stage in this book.* They are working on these skills at a higher level and on more difficult terrain than weekend skiers; but the skills are the same. And the rewards, for skiers at all levels, are the same: more control; more speed; more athletic movement; and more fun.

Amateur basketball players watch Michael Jordan's moves and try to copy them. Club tennis players watch Steffi Graf to improve their games. There is enough skiing on TV now that we can watch Tomba and Torjus and Julie Parisien and learn from their moves. If the world's best seem a little out of reach, keep M&M in mind. She's a 15-year-old girl who races in Vermont. Whatever she can do, we can do—when we learn to edge, pressure, and steer effectively.

Chapter 19

EDGE FIRST

The most effortless and efficient way to turn your skis without skidding is to apply edge angle and pressure first, then use *the smallest amount of muscular guidance that's necessary* to lure your skis into a carving response. "Lure" is Thor Kallerud's word, and a delightful choice. It asks for persuasion more than power—which is the right way to help an edged ski begin turning.

Carving at the top of the turn is best learned skiing close to the fall line and on easy terrain. The steeper the hill, and the sharper the turn, the more edge angle is required to prevent skidding when you first pressure your ski. So start where the terrain is easy, then progress to more difficult challenges.

Your goal is to begin active parallel turns with the same snow/ski/foot feel you experienced in RR turns. Move your knee inside to roll your ski on edge, pressure it lightly, and let the carve begin. Then increase edge, pressure, and steering to tighten the turn. Look at photos 50 and 51 (pages 118, 119) and imagine the position of the skiers' knees and skis just before and just after the pictures were taken. Their outside ski runs in the same groove before and after. Their CM starts over their skis, moves in a little in the photos shown, and will be still further inside in the next photo as angulation increases. Scot Schmidt shows the same skill in photo 10.

When you begin to work on this skill, let go of old habits like pushing your heels out and trying to change the direction of your skis with quick steering movements. Be patient. Instead of pushing laterally on your skis, edge them (first with knee angulation), and then add pressure and steer with the inside edge. Keep your focus on foot feel and ski response in the snow. This is precisely what Alain Villiard is doing in photo 51.

All of the above comments apply to turns that begin with moderate edging. What happens in more dynamic and aggressive skiing? Sometimes the most aggressive turns *begin* gently—feathering the ski on edge, starting the carve, then applying much stronger edge angle, pressure, and steering. When there is time, good skiers plan ahead and begin turns with a patient, progressive arc.

When hard turns must be made in short spaces, or at high speeds, additional edge and pressure are required *early in the turn*. How is this accomplished? The answer is complex, and interesting, and helps us to understand athletic skiing.

ZOOM

Edge First

Carol Merle demonstrates an extreme application of the edge first principle. For most skiing, ten to twenty degrees of edge is sufficient to begin turns with a carving action. Can you imagine the feelings Carol will have when she first comes onto the snow and her outside ski has instantaneous "edge lock?" To transition from flight to an edged and carving ski is one of the most delightful experiences in snow skiing. Recreational skiers can learn this feeling by catching a little air off a rounded knoll and landing with their outside ski fifteen or twenty degrees on edge. Trust your ski to carve and support you in the first instant it contacts the snow.

50

Karen Percy puts her ski on edge at the start of an easy turn. A subtle movement of her right knee is all that's necessary to achieve the edge angle she requires to begin this turn with a pure carving action.

51

Alain Villiard (CAN) uses knee angulation to edge his ski at the initiation of this slalom turn. Note how similar his position is to that of Karen in photo 50. Alain is approaching a gate combination set in the fall line. He does not require extreme edging or angulation here; but he is careful to start this turn with a pure carving action of his outside ski. If he skids, he slows down. If he lets his ski run on this pure, carving arc, he maintains his momentum.

DIVERGENCE / "CROSS-OVER" / "CROSS-UNDER"

A vast combination of skills are evident in athletic skiing. We need to look at one with special care. In the movement that M&M made, she moved laterally 10 feet from her right ski (60 degrees on edge) to her left ski as severely edged. It was the quickness, precision, and range of her lateral movement that astonished us. How could she do this "as easily as side-stepping a puddle?"

What questions *shouldn't* we ask? Did she lead with her inside knee? What function did her arms play? When did she turn her head? Did she use ankle roll, knee, or hip angulation? At what point in the turn was she forward, neutral, or back on her skis? What percentage of her weight was on her inside ski, and at what points in the turn? How high, or low, was her hip position? How much femoral rotation did she use? These questions could go on for pages. The answers would be interesting, but not important *because her next turn, though equally athletic, will be entirely different.*

This kind of skiing (like Michael Jordan's moves in basketball) is too complex to codify, analyze, and teach. It can only be learned by experience and experiment; and by acquiring the tools that M&M is working with. She combines edge, pressure, and steering with an efficient use of divergent lines for her body and skis. The divergence of these lines provides angulation and edge angle at the top of a turn.

Pictures explain this better than words. Look at the cover of this book. Can you imagine the edge angle Torjus had when his skis were last on the snow? Can you can see that his body is following one line (look at his eyes) and his skis another? What edge angle do you think he will have when his skis first touch the snow? Are his skis crossing under his body? Or does his body cross over his skis? Or is there some combination of both? (Look at photos 52A, B, C.)

These photos of Marc Girardelli illustrate the divergence of ski path and center of mass (CM). In photo A, Marc stands on his right ski with 50 degrees of angulation. In photo B, his skis are directly under his body. In photo C, he stands on his left ski with 30 degrees of angulation. His CM (roughly in the hip area) follows a nearly direct path toward the camera, while his skis move dramatically from his right to his left. As he moves from one turn to the next, *his skis cross under his body*. This movement is a cornerstone of athletic skiing.

PHOTOS BY THOR KALLERUD

Marc Girandelli exhibits impeccable balance, economy of motion, and relaxation in his skiing. Note how erect his upper body is, how square (not rounded) his shoulders are, and how naturally he carries his hands. His upper body movements are as natural in skiing as in running. This upper body discipline contributes to the precise control Marc has of his skis. As a racer he is focused on two goals: (1) projecting his CM on the shortest possible line; and (2) directing his skis on a rounder path that improves carving, provides angulation, and offers the stability of a carving ski for athletic movement.

52A

52B

52C

53

Photos by Thor Kallerud. Composite image by Rob Magiera

Photo 53 shows Alberto Tomba skiing the second run of the 1992 Olympic slalom—a run which he won by .59 seconds. In the five images shown, follow the line of Tomba's center of mass and the line of his skis. The photos are taken at 2/10 second intervals.

The divergence between frame 1 and frame 2 is small. This is the early part of the turn where Tomba shows patience—"edge first, then pressure." The divergence between frames 2 and 4 is much greater. Projecting his skis from the edge platform in frame 2 (right ski), he guides his skis under his body to a new edge on the left ski in frame 4. From frame 2 to frame 5, his CM follows the shortest practical line toward the next gate. (This maximizes the use of gravity for acceleration.) At the same time, his skis trace a rounder path on which carving can be maintained. (This minimizes skidding and braking.)

In summary, the CM achieves the highest velocity on the shortest line, and the skis go faster on a rounder line. The rounder line makes carving easier and reduces skidding. The line chosen for the skis determines the radius of turn they must scribe, and the amount of edge angle you will have to carve the next turn.

An athletic skier is always aware of: (1) where his skis are going, and (2) where his body is going. These are quite separate paths. Many ski technicians call the divergence of these paths a "cross-over" movement. They see that the body crosses over the skis. We prefer the term "cross-under" because it helps us to stay *ski focused* rather than body focused. This is consistent with our philosophy of skiing.

When we study balance in skiing, we learn that our body is a stable center of mass, and that our feet move around and under this stable center. With this focus, can you see how the skis accelerate under the hips from frame 2 to frame 5? The feet go further than the center of mass. When we think "cross-under," we have a better understanding of this acceleration. Our feet speed up and slow down. Our CM maintains a more constant speed.

There are times, particularly in slower speed skiing, when we "release" our bodies and let them fall to the inside of a turn. It may be more accurate to call this a "cross-over" movement. But, after letting our body go, we still direct our feet on a divergent path—to gain edge angle and begin carving the new turn. We don't want to split hairs. *We do want you to be foot conscious when you ski.* You will learn this skill more quickly if you think about your *feet crossing under* your center of mass.

This photo sequence of Tomba shows two exceptional turns. In the five images we have chosen, Tomba demonstrates a mastery of the fundamentals that win races at his level, and define good skiing at all levels. We'll refer often to this photo to illustrate a variety of skiing skills. Right now, let's focus again on the diverging paths of CM and carving ski.

How can you learn this movement? First, be sure you understand the concept. Look at drawing 17, next page.

17

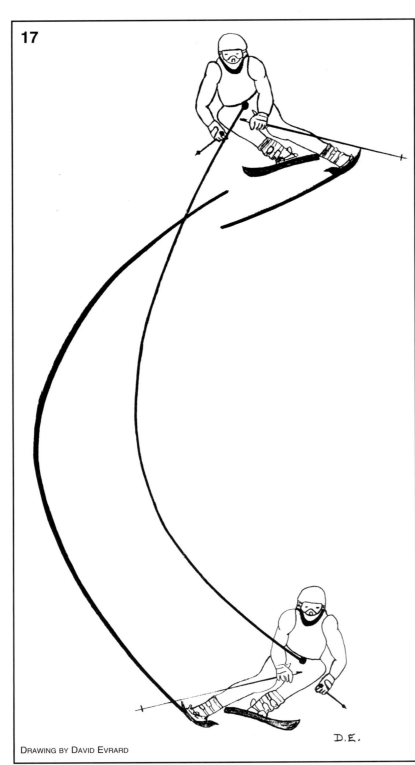

DRAWING BY DAVID EVRARD

This simple graphic shows three things: the lines converge before edge change; they diverge after edge change; and they are dramatically different. In athletic skiing, there is often a wide divergence between the line of the skis and the center of mass.

The divergence of CM and line controls edge angle at all points in a turn. *Athletic skiers show a broad divergence of these lines. Dynamic lateral movement depends on this divergence.* Milquetoast skiers, and other skidders, show little divergence. Look at the most dynamic photos in this book, and you will see over and over again that the skis are dramatically edged, and the skier's feet are "way out" from under their bodies.

To become an athletic skier—to ski with force and power, to develop carving skills—you must be comfortable with your skis "way out" from under your body. You have to learn this movement and be comfortable with it. No single exercise can teach it. In athletic skiing, each turn is a unique response to speed, terrain, and line. You don't succeed by learning one movement. You have to learn many. You start with carving and edging skills. Learn to edge before you turn. Learn to trust your skis. Then go skiing.

Be playful and see what you can do. Have an image in your mind and explore all around it. The basic move is to get your feet, with skis attached, from one side of your body to the other. This requires strong platforms to move from (cleats again). This lateral movement of your feet is just as dynamic as Jordan or Simpson making a cut. On skis it is sometimes done with independent leg action, and other times with both feet in parallel motion. When learning new movements, don't be afraid to fall down. Like a kid trying moves on a basketball court, keep trying.

LEARN FROM OTHER SPORTS.

You can learn this move in many places besides snow skiing. It's fundamental to all sports that have lateral movement. We suggest the following:

Take a ride on your bicycle, and on a gentle downhill make a long series of "swooping turns". See how far you can lean on the bicycle and not fall over. Link turns as close together as you can with as much lean as you can.

As a skier, what can you learn from this exercise? No two turns are exactly the same. You are light on the seat when the tires change edge. You feel heavy in the seat in the belly of the turn. Your tires can't be skidding when you make a dynamic move. Most important, you can sense the rhythm of lateral movement as your feet move under your body. Your feet and center of mass move constantly on divergent paths. Do your wheels cross under your body? Or does your body cross over your wheels? Or some combination of both?

Next put on your in-line skates. Choose a gentle slope and make the same kind of turns you made on the bicycle. In-line skates force you to carve. The balance, anticipation, edge change, and weight shift are much like skiing.

If left to play long enough on in-line skates, what sort of turns will you make? Feet close together. Feet wide apart. Feet diverging. Stepping turns. All the ways you can turn on skis, you can turn on skates. Do you lead some turns with your inside knee? Do you turn with different percentages of weight on your inside and outside skate? Do you use your arms for balance and power? All these different moves are seen in racing technique. You do them naturally on skates. Tomba does them naturally on skis. When you learn to control edge and pressure as well as he does, the same variety of movement comes naturally to your skiing.

Next try ice skates. Again we are working on carving edges. We can move inside and know our edges will support us—just as the bicycle tires did, the road skates did, and your skis will when you carve.

Try water skiing. A slalom ski with its deep fin provides wonderful carving actions. You learn a variety of banking and balancing skills—leaning into the turn and knowing the ski edge will support you and turn under your body. In short line slalom, the CM and the ski path are widely divergent. (See photo 54.)

Steve and Phil Mahre are enthusiastic water skiers. Bob and Chris La Point, who have been world champion water skiers, are equally enthusiastic snow skiers. Do they learn from one sport and apply their lessons to another. You bet they do!

HELP? Have Witherell and Evrard gone mad? Are they trying to teach advanced snow skiing by talking about other sports? Absolutely! *Athletic skiing is athletic movement.* It can be learned in many ways.

To learn athletic movement, you must be free from all constraints of self-conscious "technique." *You learn by exploration and innovation.* Watch a child or an NBA player fooling around and shooting baskets. They are always "playing." Imagination and creativity are delightfully evident in the warm-up routines at NBA games. They are equally evident if you go to the training hill at Burke and watch the academy kids.

Racers don't advance their skiing in the same ways that pupils in ski school classes do—following an instructor and trying to learn a designated turn. Racers play with terrain, search for speed, look for better balance, explore the limits of lateral motion, set their own goals, play with their edges. They watch one another, seeking inspiration. They're dynamic, spontaneous, imaginative, creative.

Those who are winning races are simply more athletic than those who are slower. They have better "cleats." They find better ways to get the edge they need and to apply the right amount of pressure. They move more dynamically. They choose a better line.

Fall training programs for racers include a variety of obstacle course training. They have rope mazes, dry-land slalom, and other tasks that demand powerful lateral movement. They learn edging, angulation, upper and lower-body independence, cross-over and cross-under skills. If offered a choice to train in sneakers or soccer shoes, they always choose cleats. Cleats provide better platforms for lateral movement. They are more akin to skiing for those whose carving skills are strong.

54

TOM KING

In water ski slalom, the ski path and CM follow widely divergent lines. Helena Kjellander won the Women's Slalom at the 1991 and 1993 World Water Ski Championships. As a developing athlete in Sweden, she was an outstanding alpine ski racer. Warren Witherell has coached Helena since 1986.

We'll end this chapter by returning to the bicycle. Let's think again about the freedom for lateral movement we have on a bike—leaning alternately left and right and combining cross-under and cross-over as we swoop from turn to turn with the tires always carving. We have speed with control, and it's exhilarating.

Now park the bicycle, and sit on a tricycle. What changes? On the tricycle, you can't get your feet out from under you. You can't angulate. You can't generate as much pressure on your tires. You can't edge. You can't turn sharp at high speed without tipping over. In short, you can't have as much fun. (See photos 55 and 56.)

55

56

On facing page, Whitney Wertz "puts her wheels on edge" and leans into the turn. She is obviously having fun. Above, Bucky Brownell is having difficulty leaning to the inside of the turn. He can't get his wheels on their inside edge; his angulation and lateral movement are restricted; his speeds are limited; and his facial expression suggests he is having less fun than Whitney. A pertinent story accompanies this photograph. Whitney's younger brother was asked to ride the tricycle for these photos. Having recently learned to ride a bike, he refused. He asserted he didn't do three wheelers anymore. Children understand. The freedom of lateral movement is appealing to all athletes!

What can be done better on three wheels than two? At slow speeds, balance is easier. You're more stable when sand or pebbles are on the road (you skid but don't fall). In every sense, the tricycle is like skiing on a flat ski. Your CM stays over your feet. Lateral movements are impossible. Angulation is restricted. You're uncomfortable with speed. (See photo 57.)

TEAM RUSSELL

The skiers shown here are Gary and Debra Moore. Both are strong, all-mountain skiers from Aspen. In this photo they are imitating novice skiers for an advertising brochure. All they have done is limit themselves to five degrees of edging. When deprived of the carving skills and edge platforms they normally depend on, they are forced to skid, their posture becomes defensive, and their skiing becomes static.

Do these skiers remind you of riding a tricycle? They have little angulation or inward lean. Their hips are behind their feet. Their speed is slow. ***Compared to all the other photos in this book, this skiing looks dreadfully static.*** The body positions are ski school perfect; but the skiing is boring. There is no athletic engagement, and no potential for it. On a skidding ski, you'll always be static because balance is tentative.

Only from a carving ski is dynamic movement possible. Look again at frame 2 of the Tomba sequence. If his right ski was flat on the snow and skidding, what could he do?

And where could he go? He would slide sideways, basically out of control. Because his ski is carving, and provides a platform for dynamic movement, he can project his body and his skis across the hill on exactly the lines he chooses. Frame 2 shows us "cleats." Frames 3, 4, and 5 show what we can do with cleats. It is this movement that gives life to athletic skiing.

Before leaving the Tomba sequence, take a long look at image 5. Imagine how much fun you could have skiing from positions like this. Tomba has tremendous grip on the snow with *both* skis and they are nearly 60 degrees on edge. Both skis are carving and provide solid platforms for projection into the next turn. This is really fun!

When you were a kid, you couldn't wait to graduate from tricycle to bicycle. As a skier, you should be just as anxious to progress from skidding to carving—from static skiing to dynamic skiing.

58

Chapter 20

PRESSURE

Pressure controls the shape of a ski when pressed into reverse camber. As ski shape changes, so does the arc of a carved turn. Many of the photos in this book show skis in reverse camber.

It is obvious that controlling pressure is a critical factor in carving. How much pressure? Applied with what timing, and what method? Forward, centered, or aft on the ski? For how long? There are no simple answers. Carving is always dynamic. Pressure and ski response are constantly changing.

The best way to think of pressure is to think of being "light" or "heavy" on your skis. The purpose of pressure is simple: to bend the ski into reverse camber. The amount of bend you get depends on the flex of your skis, the nature of the snow (hard or soft), the amount of side-cut in your skis, the amount the ski is rolled on edge, and how much steering force you use. Speed plays a big role in all turns because pressure increases with speed for any turn of a constant radius. Every change of turning arc changes pressure as well.

There are many ways we help students to more actively control pressure. First, we ask them to think about pressure as a line on an oscilloscope—always moving up and down, with infinite variety, with changing highs and lows, and with changing distance between the peaks. Depending on the terrain and talent of our skiers, we ask them to ski in ways that would make specific patterns on the oscilloscope: "Try to make the highs and lows further from the mid-line." "Let's make the waves longer, or shorter." "Make ten turns where each turn has a distinctively different pressure pattern." These exercises help people to be aware of their movement in new ways.

When working with the oscilloscope image, it's important to remind students that the receptors providing information to the scope are *under their feet*. The scope records the pressure on the soles of their feet. This image helps students to be snow, ski, boot, and foot conscious whenever they think about pressure.

There are two primary ways that skiers change the pressure on their skis. The more obvious is by raising and lowering their CM—"weighting" and "unweighting" as ski technicians have long taught us. For recreational skiing at slower speeds, and for slalom turns close to the fall line, raising and lowering the CM is a primary method of pressure control. As our speed and lateral motion expand, weighting and unweighting occur on increasingly diagonal planes.

In GS and Super G skiing, and whenever carving skills are strong, the primary instrument of pressure control is the adjustment of turn radius. Pressure can be increased by tightening the radius of a turn which increases the centrifugal force of your body against your skis. When turn radius is lengthened, pressure is decreased.

To understand, look again at the Tomba photos (page 120). Previously, we focused on the divergence of his skis and center of mass. Look now at the variations in pressure. He is light in frame 1. Heavy in frame 2. Off the snow in 3. Light in 4. And heavy again in 5. In your mind's eye, can you add frames between those shown and compute the pressure Tomba uses? Is he thinking about pressuring his skis? Or does he "just do it?"

Though Tomba skis instinctively, the proprioceptors in his feet are always busy reporting to his brain and central nervous system. As this information is processed, Tomba adjusts the pressure on his skis and changes the arc they will carve. This is a complex, intuitive process. We don't have to diagram it with force vectors. We do need an image of the process.

In which frame of the sequence does the pressure increase dramatically on his right ski? Clearly it is frame 2. Has Tomba extended his hips here or raised his center of mass? No. The pressure builds because his skis turn under his body. If his skis were flat and skidding, there would be few changes in pressure. Because his skis are edged and carving, there are large changes in pressure.

Through the precise use of edge, pressure, and subtle steering, Tomba starts his right ski carving in frame 1. He increases edge angle and steering forces just before frame 2. As the ski begins to turn more sharply to the left, the pressure builds quickly. This added pressure creates more reverse camber > a sharper turn > still more reverse camber > and a still sharper turn. This is a simple chain reaction in which small initial forces lead inevitably to the creation of stronger ones. ***This subtle process is the dominant pressure control system in high speed, athletic skiing.*** The same process works from frame 4 (initial edging of his ski) to frame 5 where the ski is heavily loaded.

As your carving skills expand, so does your ability to control pressure by changing turn radius. This is a *very important* concept for athletic skiing. Racers are working hard to more fully understand, develop, and exploit this ability. It has important applications to carving at the start of a turn which is so important for recreational skiers as well as racers.

Pressure control is a dynamic skill. It's harder to teach than edging skills. You can apply 10 degrees of edge, and hold it. You can see angles and measure them. Pressure is more variable, and harder to see and measure. It takes more imagination to teach and learn. We often ask students to talk aloud as they ski—using words like "Press >> Release >> Press >> Release." Or for longer turns, "Press, Press >>> Float >>> Press, Press >>> Float." We say the words with them and help them to feel the rhythm and timing in specific cadences. For short, quick turns, we use words like "sting" and "pop." We ask them to ski as different birds fly—swooping and gliding like a hawk, or moving quickly like a songbird. These imaginary games build variety and flexibility in their skiing.

One of the best ways to experiment with pressure is to sing while you ski and dance to your music. Try the "Blue Danube Waltz" for half a mile, then switch to any of your favorites. Try a slow, rhythmic tempo; then a jazzy, upbeat piece. Ski as you feel. Dance on skis as you would dance anywhere else, enjoying the rhythm and freedom of movement.

Think of the free skating programs you see in the Olympics. The best feature a variety of music. Parts of each program are flowing and melodic. Other parts are quick and energetic. The best skaters are wonderfully athletic and imaginative. They "play" to all kinds of music. You can choreograph your ski runs the same way. Select music that's appropriate for terrain. Express emotion in your skiing. Can you ski happy or sad? Melancholy or carefree?

The challenge of skiing is not to get from the top of the mountain to the bottom, or to make turns in perfect form. It is to be fully alive, to be artistic and free, to express many moods and feelings. The figure skaters got it right when they threw compulsory figures out of their competitions. "The best skater is the best free skater," they said. Bravo! And what do they measure in free skating? Athleticism <> Creativity <> Power <> Grace <> Courage <> Humor <> Playfulness <> Variety <> A complete mastery of their tools and environment. They celebrate the joy and the magic of human movement; and *they do it on carving edges*. They only skid sideways when it's time to stop. We should ski the same way.

When we master edge and pressure, we can ski with the rhythm and grace of Torvil and Dean, or the power and precision of Gretsky and Lemieux. Or of Tomba and M&M. For us, skiing is better than skating. Our playing fields are tilted so we coast downhill. We play with gravity. Our acceleration is free. We have the sky for our roof, and always fresh air. Is there any better sport in the world?

Chapter 21

STEERING

While researching this book, we reviewed a hundred definitions of steering. All expressed *some* truth; but excluded *all* of it. One instructor in Vermont got it right. Here's the definition, and we ask everyone in skiing to accept it:

> **"Steering: After you edge and pressure a ski, steering is everything else you do that applies a twisting force to your ski."**

We like this definition for two reasons. First, it begins with the qualifier "after edge and pressure." And second, it makes no attempt to define specific body movements. "All the other things you do" includes *everything*—foot twist, femoral rotation, blocking, or even sticking one arm out in the wind.

PSIA has tried for years to separate "steering" from "rotary control." In our experience, we have yet to find two instructors who agree on where "steering" ends and "rotary" begins. The lines are impossibly vague. If a ski is dead flat and you twist your foot, a "pivot" occurs. If the ski is carving cleanly, the same twisting force at the foot encourages the ski to tighten its arc. What if the ski is a little on edge? If a ski is mostly carving, but skidding a little, is femoral rotation "steering" or "rotary"? Rotary control specialists will argue for days. We think it doesn't matter.

We seldom talk about rotation when teaching skiing. When "rotation" is used, the focus of the mind is on the body. When "steering" is used, the focus is on turning the ski. That's better. Words, and their connotations, are important.

For ski instruction, "steering" is the best word. To *steer* is to be active and precise in directing a moving object. You steer a car or a bobsled. To *rotate* is passive and imprecise. You rotate a lazy susan or a pig on a spit.

If you focus on rotary forces and teach rotary movements, as sure as snow is white you'll depend on them in your skiing. If you focus on steering forces—as *supplements* to edge and pressure—you'll do less skidding.

Whenever you think about steering, remember what was said in Chapter 12 about steering forces acting on the plane of the ski base, not the plane of the snow. Steering *an edged ski* increases pressure on the front of the ski and helps it to carve at the start of a turn. To reinforce this image, refer again to drawing 13 on page 74.

When you can't get a ski to carve as sharp a turn as you want, the first thing you do is provide "muscular guidance" to the edged ski. The last thing you do is jump in the air and rotate with all available resources. Steering is both of these movements and everything in between. This is true whether you are racing, powder skiing, or working your way through bumps.

Rotation of the human body is as instinctive as breathing. Babies learn to rotate before they learn to crawl. Why should we teach rotation, or even think about it, on skis? Carving on skis is a learned skill, and must be taught. Rotation is instinctive, and need not be taught.

If beginners are placed on skis with no instruction, they first try to turn with rotation. It takes them a *long* time to figure out carving. Without specific instruction, few would ever figure it out. The *exception* is those who have experience with carving on water skis or skates. Their bodies *know* the feel and efficiencies of carving. If not confused by other instructions, they will try to carve on snow.

Nearly every student we teach has a long history of skidding turns and using rotation. They don't have to *learn* rotary skills. They need to *unlearn* them. Youngsters who come to racing programs with a "heel-push habit" are difficult to reprogram.

Harald Harb, PSIA D-Team member and long-time racing coach, says "coaches don't have to teach rotary to racers. Racers get more rotary force than they want, from femoral rotation and tibial torsion. The problem for racers is to control rotary forces."

This is also the problem for recreational "skidders" who are learning to carve. Even with RR turns, it takes a long time to get skiers to edge and pressure their skis and just stand on them—with no heel push, no foot steer, and no upper body rotation. If you want to ski fast and leave narrow tracks, you must use steering as a supplement to edge and pressure. In every way possible, use ski design to create turning forces.

INTERLUDE

Before moving on to the second half of this book, we should review again the traits of an athletic skier that were outlined in Chapter 2.

1. Exceptional Balance
2. Dynamic Motion
3. Carving Skills
4. Lateral Movement
5. Strength
6. Quickness and Agility
7. Economy of Motion
8. Relaxation
9. A Natural and Unaffected Style
10. Playfulness and Imagination

These descriptions should have more meaning now than when you began reading. For example, having learned about boot fit and leg alignment, has your understanding of "Balance" been advanced? As you better understand carving and having cleats, does "Quickness and Agility" take on new dimensions? Can you see how important "Lateral Movement" is in athletic skiing?

Each of the photos in Chapter 2 should "tell" you more now than the first time you looked at them. This is not a book to read once and put on a shelf. The longer you study it, the more you will understand. Good coaches watch the same films many times, always learning something new. Often they watch a racer for weeks or months before connecting one movement to another and better understanding the whole. That's the way to read this book. One page or chapter adds perspective to another. One picture helps us to see what others can teach.

In the sections ahead, we'll address the special interests of physical training, instructors, racers, and coaches. Our understanding of skiing is enriched by each of these perspectives. There is no knowledge that helps only one kind of skier. Good skiing is good skiing, anywhere on the mountain.

"Power Buys Freedom"

PART 6

TRAINING FOR ATHLETIC SKIING

Skiing is one of the most demanding of all athletic activities—requiring a broad combination of strength, balance, athleticism, and skills. Skiers must combine sport specific training with a broad based fitness program. The physiological base which supports the sport of skiing includes:

1. Aerobic Capacity
2. Anaerobic Capacity
3. Quickness and Agility
4. Strength and Power
5. Muscle Endurance
6. Flexibility
7. Coordination
8. Balance

We'll look at the most important components of a sound training program in the next five chapters.

SKI FAST— LEAVE NARROW TRACKS!

CARTOON BY VIKI FLECKENSTEIN WOODWORTH

In the space available, we can provide only a brief introduction to this important subject. We hope many readers will be inspired to improve their training programs and to expand their knowledge of training principles.

We encourage all athletes to keep a training log. You have a better chance of reaching your goals if you know where you have been and where you are going. You develop this skill by keeping good training logs. These can be quite simple or very detailed, but they must be legible and include some basic information. You must record the date, kind of activity, duration, intensity, number of repetitions, and, if possible, moods for each training day or session. Other information you might want to record includes the number of hours of sleep you had, and your resting heart rate in the morning before rising.

Readers who wish to learn more about training for skiing should read the *1993 U.S. Ski Team Alpine Training Manual*. This is an excellent guide to all aspects of training.*

---

* USST, P.O. Box 100, Park City, UT 84060. (801) 649-9090
  ($15.00)

Chapter 22

STRENGTH TRAINING

C arving skills and athletic skiing can be learned by any man, woman, or child who meets reasonable standards for coordination and strength. You don't have to be a super-jock to use edge, pressure, and steering; or to learn cross-over and cross-under skills. The athletic skiing we promote is efficient and relaxing when used in the "cruising mode."

There are, however, additional rewards for stronger athletes who ski in the "power mode." Strength is basic to all sport movements; and the effective use of strength is one of the most important factors in performance skiing. Athletes who wish to play at the upper end of the performance spectrum must pay their dues in strength training. Whether skiing powder or crud, attacking a bump field, or tightening the radius of a high-speed turn, you can do more and do it better if you have sufficient power. *Power buys freedom.*

TRAINING FOR STRENGTH

Carefully planned weight training programs provide a foundation for the development of *strength*. These programs must be tailored to the age and physical development of each athlete. As there are many excellent books on weight training, and available instructors at most gyms, we'll skip the details here.

TRAINING FOR POWER

Skiing requires dynamic strength, which is more accurately called "power." Power is the ability to apply maximum force in the shortest period of time. Work = Force × Distance ÷ Time. Weight training, plyometrics, leg routines, hill bounding, interval running, circuit training, and interval bike hill sprints are common methods of training for power. All of these methods are incorporated in sound fitness programs that are sport specific for alpine skiing.

INTERVAL TRAINING

For interval training, where an intense exercise period is followed by a period of rest, the work periods appropriate to skiing vary from 30 to 180 seconds. Monitoring your heart rate is important during interval training. A reading of 170–180 beats per minute (BPM) during the work period represents an intensity level of 85–90 percent for a typical athlete. It is not unusual to see heart rates approaching 200 BPM during the work phase. It is important to let your heart rate recover to 120 BPM during rest phases. These rest phases should be nearly the same duration as the work phase, or possibly longer if necessary to recover. (See information on heart rate awareness in Chapter 26.)

The most intense periods for interval and circuit training should be scheduled for the last six to eight weeks before on snow training begins. Quickness, agility, coordination, and balance can all be developed in interval training programs. For instance, rather than do interval hill sprints on a straight road, do them running in the woods, or around cones, or wherever there is uneven terrain.

PLYOMETRIC TRAINING

Plyometrics is a form of power training that encompasses a broad range of bounding and rebounding skills. All manner of hopping, leaping, and jumping drills train the body to react more quickly and to rebound more powerfully. Photo 59A shows the plyometric training benches at Burke Mountain Academy. Both one and two-legged drills are performed from these benches—always jumping to the ground and rebounding as quickly as possible to the next platform. Significant gains in quickness of motor nerve and muscle response can be made with plyometric training. An imaginative athlete can create many plyometric drills. Detailed information on plyometrics is available in numerous books and in the Fall 1992 issue of the *American Ski Coach*.

59A

TOM DeCARLO

TOM DECARLO

To make this exercise increasingly difficult, the athletes slide the shock cords higher up the poles. When the cords are low, quickness is rewarded. When the cords and high, power is required with each jump.

The plyometric training benches at BMA. The benches are almost waist high, and provide serious challenges to the athletes. It is most impressive to see the stronger athletes run the whole series of benches on one leg.

FAVORITE EXERCISES

In designing a training program, there are many more good exercises to choose from than any athlete has time to do. Variety is important; but a few basic exercises are par-

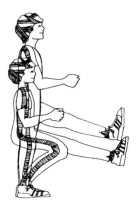

1 LEG KNEE BENDS: (30 each leg) Standing on one leg, opposite leg forward, hands in skiing position, sink slowly to 90 degree bend; rise again slowly.

LATERAL THRUSTS: (40) Leap to the side from outside leg to outside leg. A leap in each direction counts as one.

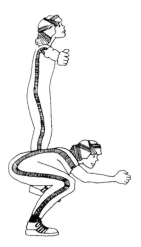

DOWNHILL JUMPS: (30) Low tuck position, leap as high as possible, land and repeat immediately.

HIGH BOUNCING: (2 minutes) Upright position, feet together, arms held in a skiing position and quiet. Leap as high as possible and as fast as possible when bringing the knees up on each jump. Variations include bouncing from side to side and forward to backward. May also be done on one leg.

Drawings are reprinted from the USST Alpine Training Manual

ticularly helpful in preparing for skiing. Ten of our favorites are shown here. The numbers in parenthesis indicate the maximum number of repetitions for each exercise. Most skiers will begin with half this number or even less, building gradually until they can do a full routine by the end of fall training.

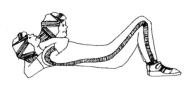

CRUNCHES: (60) Lying on back, hands behind head, legs extended, curl upper body and knees up over the abdomen, repeat.

CRAMPS, ISOMETRIC: (60) Lying on back, hands behind head, knees bent. Curl shoulders up, hold for 10 sec. while breathing.

SIDE UPS: (40 each side) Lying on side, hands behind head, feet and knees held down. Raise upper body as far as possible.

TRUNK LIFTS: (15 slowly) Lie prone on table with lower body from hips down on table, upper body hangs over end of table, hands behind head. Lower upper body to vertical position Slowly raise upper body until parallel with table top. Do not raise to arched back position.

LATERAL LEG RAISE: (40 each side) Lying on side, raise leg laterally as follows:

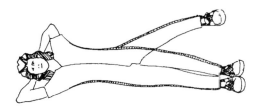

(1) 10 single leg

(2) 10 both legs

Chapter 23

Principles of Training

We haven't the space here to outline specific training programs for the wide variety of readers of this book. There are, however, principles of training that apply to all athletes. These principles should serve as guidelines for all forms of training. You should understand the following:

1. Individual Response
2. Adaptation
3. Warm Up, Cool Down
4. Progression
5. Overload
6. Specificity
7. Variety
8. Reversibility

INDIVIDUAL RESPONSE

Athletes respond differently to the same training for various reasons. These reasons include heredity, maturity, nutrition, amount of rest, level of fitness, motivation, environmental influences, and disease or injury. Get to know yourself as an athlete. You must learn about your strengths and weaknesses.

ADAPTATION

As an athlete trains, subtle changes take place in the body as it adapts to the added demands that are placed on it. It takes weeks, months, and even years of patient, hard work to achieve success. Rushing things invites injury and illness. Some of the subtle improvements you will see are improved cardiovascular-respiratory function (aerobic capacity), and improved muscular strength and endurance (anaerobic capacity). Only as the body (or parts of the body) adapt to certain loads should increased demands be placed on it.

WARM UP, COOL DOWN

A warm up routine should precede all workouts. Calisthenics, light jogging, and jumping rope are great ways to raise your core temperature. These should be followed by passive and active stretching. A good warm up improves performance and prevents injuries. A cool down period ends each workout as the body temperature is brought down slowly. Stretching after a workout helps to remove metabolic wastes and to reduce muscle soreness.

PROGRESSION

The amount and intensity of exercise should be gradually increased each week, month, and year. This allows the body to adapt gradually to the increased stress of exercise. When training loads are increased too quickly, the body can't adapt, and instead breaks down. Progression is concerned with *frequency, intensity,* and *duration* of work outs.

OVERLOAD

A training program must place increasing demands on the body for improvement to take place. With sensitivity to the principles of *adaptation* and *progression*, the body must be subjected to increasing amounts of work. The body will only improve in performance if the *intensity* of exercise is gradually increased. *Frequency* and *duration* of work-outs must also be considered in planning overload.

SPECIFICITY

Performance improves most when the training is specific to the activity. The closer to the ski season, the more specific the training should be. Although the transfer is not perfect, many dry land activities can simulate skiing. If you imagine yourself on skis when doing this training, your excitement for the coming season will rise, and training will be more fun. (See Viki's cartoon on page 139.) She says this portrays her thinking during fall training.

VARIETY

For psychological as well as physiological reasons, variation in training is important. From the psychological standpoint, when work-outs become dull, productivity drops. Do something different to eliminate boredom. From a physiological point, it is usually best to have a short work-out followed by a long one, and an intense workout followed by an easier one.

REVERSIBILITY

Unfortunately, most physiological gains from intense training are reversible. It may take three times as long to gain endurance as to lose it. With complete inactivity, fitness has been shown to decline about 10 percent per week. Although strength may decline a bit more slowly, inactivity results in muscle atrophy in even the best-trained athletes. During the off-season, or transition periods, a maintenance program must be followed to reduce the effects of reversibility. This is called "active rest." A lack of general physical training during the ski season will cause a decline as well, which is why winter maintenance programs are important.

Chapter 24

CROSS-TRAINING

The more diversified our training, the more fun we can have as athletes, and the less likely we are to become bored or stale. Following are brief descriptions of the training modes that are most productive for serious skiers.

IN-LINE SKATING

This activity is more closely related to skiing than any other form of training. You can simulate skiing going downhill (photo 60A), and condition your body going uphill (60B). The muscle contractions and body movements used in skating are closely related to skiing. This is not the case with running or biking.

60A

Tina Vindum

In-line skating develops a well balanced stance with a flexed-knee position that is supple and dynamic. As there's no phantom foot, you must stay centered fore and aft (or get road rash). A good stance on skates is similar to a good stance on skis.

When going downhill, the wheels grip the pavement much like the edge of a carving ski. The sensation of the turn resembles that of a clean arc on snow and utilizes subtle pressure changes from toe to heel. Skating develops a balanced lateral motion of the legs. The

Tina Vindum

60B

weight transfer from turn to turn is gradual and integrated. Ski poles are optional and provide good parallels to movement on skis. Specific technical skills such as diverging steps are easily taught on skates and transfer quickly to skiing. Slalom courses can be set with highway cones or by putting tape on the road. (photo 61)

ERIK OSTLING

David Evrard runs cone slalom. Note the similarities of stance and movement patterns between skating and skiing.

Many National Team athletes train intensively on in-line skates during the summer season. When watching World Cup teams free ski in 1993, we were surprised at the number of lateral movements that mirrored skating. In playful, relaxed skiing, these movements were more evident than a few years ago—before in-line skating became popular. Good athletes transfer skills quite naturally from one sport to another.

A wide variety of skate designs are now available. "Slalom skates" are an obvious choice for alpine skiers; but five-wheel road skates and other special designs offer interesting choices for different kinds of training.

RUNNING

Running is an easy way to train because it requires little equipment and can be done almost anywhere. Most people look at running as training for an aerobic base, but other training goals can be met as well. Anaerobic conditioning results from interval and circuit-type training as well as from sprints and work periods of a short, explosive nature. Dry land slalom drills (photos 62 and 63) provide many parallels to skiing. Courses can be set to emphasize quickness, agility, lateral movement, and selection of line. Lateral movement and all similarities to skiing are enhanced if soccer shoes are worn.

TOM DeCARLO

Burke student, Chip Knight, develops power and lateral movement skills running dryland slalom in the school's sand pit. Chip was Gold Medalist in Slalom at the 1993 World Junior Championships.

63

TOM DECARLO

Gusty Swift runs a dryland course that is set to emphasize quickness and agility.

Side hill running is especially good for developing lateral strength and balance. The lateral muscles in the foot, ankle, knee, and hip all work under severe loads when skiing. Most weight training, biking, and road running neglect these muscles. We recommend running and hiking on uneven terrain whenever possible.

BIKING

The bike is an excellent cross-training tool for skiing. Used correctly, it provides an ideal workout for developing power and endurance in the large leg muscles. It is ideally suited for both aerobic and anaerobic conditioning. Most athletes find biking is more fun than running.

Mountain biking is a favorite training activity for many skiers. We prefer it over road biking because it is more sport specific for alpine skiing. Excellent balance and total body control are required for mountain biking. (See photo 64.) Athletes learn to look ahead and adjust to terrain changes. Lateral and diagonal muscles are used in ways supportive to skiing needs.

A mountain bike provides excellent conditioning for the anaerobic energy system. Typical tasks in mountain biking raise the heart rate to levels similar to those in skiing; and also offer periods of rest. It is wise to change the intensity of your workload by sprinting on hills, and recovering on easy sections. The versatility of an athlete is continually challenged when biking on difficult terrain.

Tina Vindum rides on the rocks at Moab, Utah. A multi-sport athlete, Tina has won National Championship medals in both mountain biking and in-line skating.

64

LARRY PROSER

GAMES: FORMAL AND INFORMAL COMPETITION

Playing games and competing on an informal basis is the most fun way to train and condition yourself in the off season. We highly encourage this kind of training. Our favorite activities are: ice or roller hockey, soccer, water skiing, gymnastics, tennis, raquetball, squash, volley ball, basketball, hacky sack, rock climbing, and bike racing.

STRETCHING

While stretching is not a form of cross training, a consistent stretching program supports *all* forms of training activity. Flexibility and relaxation exercises are important to any fitness program. Learn to stretch properly! When stretching, relax and breath *slowly*, increasing your stretches slightly as you exhale. *Do not* hold your breath. You should feel a slight pull in your muscles in order to gain any benefit, but this should never be painful. Hold each stretch for 20–30 seconds to gain the most benefit. Stretch all areas of your body from your neck to your ankles. Concentrate on the muscle groups you have worked hardest on that particular day.

Nearly all top athletes are aware of the benefits of stretching and flexibility exercises. They are important for at least four reasons:

1. Flexibility exercises increase the length of your muscles which reduces the chance of muscle injuries in training or competition.

2. Stretching exercises relax the muscles after strenuous workouts. This increases the flow of vital substances through the muscles to clean waste products produced during exercise. Increased circulation replenishes and repairs muscle tissue.

3. Stretching enhances performance. Athletes perform better when their muscles are flexible and relaxed than when they are tight or stiff.

4. Stretching after a hard workout *feels* good. After stretching for 10–20 minutes, your muscles relax which in turn relaxes your mind, helping you to feel better both physically and mentally. You feel refreshed and more energetic! You also sleep better.

It takes time to become flexible. Be patient but persistent! Regularity is important in stretching as in all training. Some days you will feel tighter than others. Accept this and don't stretch harder. Over time, a good stretching program will help you to be more flexible and to feel more fit and alive.

Chapter 25

IMPROVING BALANCE

Everyone *talks* about balance, but few people *do* something about it. It is well understood that balance (good or bad) is an inherited trait, and some people are more blessed than others. It is less understood that balance can be improved through training. The body learns by doing.

Balance is the ability to maintain equilibrium as body positions continually change. As with strength and endurance training, performance is enhanced by asking the body to accept increasingly difficult tasks.

Balance can be improved by fence walking, curb walking, rock hopping, balance beam work (photo 65), tight rope walking, and all other activities that require balancing as a central task. Walking, hiking, and running on side hills and uneven terrain provide constant challenges for lateral balance. These are good activities to develop balance for skiing.

When we first think about balance, we think of a hidden, internal mechanism that works in secret ways. Indeed, the brain and central nervous system (CNS) are invisible computers. But who does their work? Muscles! Muscles continually support good balance; and provide recovery from imbalance. If you think carefully about balancing tasks in skiing, what muscles are most important? Let's think about this on the fore/aft and lateral planes.

FORE/AFT BALANCE

Skiing offers constant challenges to maintain balance on the fore/aft plane. If you get in the back seat, what muscles are needed to recover? *Abdominal muscles*. All training programs for racing set high priorities on abdominal strength. "Killer stomach routines" are regular fare at Burke Mountain Academy. Only leg strength gets more attention in the training program.

In dynamic skiing on uneven terrain, fore/aft balance is in continual flux. Abdominal muscles, *and the opposing muscles in the lower back*, are always busy. For all fitness training, it's important to develop balanced muscle groups. If you train to have extra strong abdominals, you must work equally hard on the muscles of the lower back. These, too, are needed to support the upper body in dynamic skiing.

65

TOM DeCARLO

Kirsten Richardson / Becky Young

LATERAL BALANCE

Skiing places high demands on the muscles that support lateral balance. What muscles are these, and how well do we train them? Some careful thought is required here. Think of the specific lateral, diagonal, and rotational forces we encounter in skiing. The muscles that support these movements are not well trained in traditional strength programs. Running, leg squats, quadricep extensions, biking, arm curls, bench presses, etc., all work on fore and aft planes. Few weight machines, in even the most sophisticated gyms, train lateral or rotary muscles. For skiing, these must be trained.

For the big muscles of the abdomen and back, all exercises should be done with diagonal components. In addition to straight sit-ups and trunk lifts, do diagonal ones etc. Most skiers are conscious of these needs. There are smaller muscles in the foot, ankle and lower leg that are important for balance in skiing but are seldom well trained. What are these?

Let's start at the ankle and work up. How strong are your feet and ankles on a rotary axis? To find out, have a partner hold your foot while you try to twist it. Do ten repetitions of five seconds each—first with your knee straight, and again with your knee bent.

Most skiers will find these muscles are surprisingly weak. We encourage a complete set of partner exercises to develop foot/ankle strength on rotary and fore/aft planes. The ski is a powerful lever. The muscles of the foot and ankle are the weakest link in the chain that connects our bodies to our skis. Many foot-twist exercises can be done by simply holding your own feet and twisting against your hands.

The *tibialis anterior* is the long muscle that runs up the front of your shin bone. If you put your heel on the ground, and lift your forefoot toward your shin, this is the muscle you use. In skiing, large demands are placed on this muscle. Few people train it. In the gym, we use the machine for hamstring curls. Sit upright facing the foot pads, hook your feet under the pads, and do curls with your fore/foot. Partner exercises are good too; or hook your toes under a bed and lift.

As you think about the demands of skiing, you can identify other muscles in your body that work on lateral and diagonal planes to support good balance. When these muscles are strengthened, your balance on skis improves.

CROSS-TRAINING

It is evident that balance is a function of total athleticism as well as genetics. Many kinds of training support and improve our balance. Quickness supports balance and can be improved through plyometric training and agility exercises. All sports that involve extensive lateral movement (such as soccer, tennis, and in-line skating) are helpful in developing the muscles that support balance in skiing.

Mountain biking demands the most complex balancing skills and develops both strength and proprioception. Running in dry stream beds, on uneven terrain, and down mountains requires physical balancing, good depth perception, and eye/foot coordination skills.

The eyes are our number one source for balance information. Depth perception is especially important for skiers. Recent research shows the eyes can be trained to improve depth perception. Athletes working with these concepts report significant performance gains. All skiers know they ski better in clear sunlight than in cloud. As visual acuity decreases, balance responses are impaired. This tells us that skiing with the best possible lenses for specific light conditions will improve our balance and performance. Skiers who are "looking for an edge" should pay more attention to the importance of the eyes in balance functions.*

It is clear there is more to balance than genetics.

*See "Train the Eyes to Ski Better," Robert J. LaMarche. *Snow Country* magazine, October, 1993.

Chapter 26

HEART RATE, REST, AND HYDRATION

HEART RATE

In your development as an athlete, you should learn how to use your heart rate (pulse) to help in your training. Most coaches say you should work in the 150–160 BPM range. This defines the *intensity* you should work at. This is often called a "target training zone" with the low side for low-intensity days and the high side for high-intensity days.

The best time to take your pulse is right after waking up in the morning. After a period of time you will notice a pattern. This is your "resting pulse," or resting heart rate. Any radical swings in your RHR indicates you might be over-training. To establish your "target training zone," take your age and subtract it from 220. Multiply this number by 70% and then by 90%. Some people say your target zone should be 65%–85%. Anywhere in this range is fine.

For example: If you are   15 years old: 220 − 15 = 205
                          205 × .70 = 143.5 rounded off = 144 BPM
                          205 × .90 = 184.5 rounded off = 185 BP
                          Your target zone is: 144 to 185.

If this athlete's pulse falls below 144 when working out, he isn't working hard enough. If his pulse goes above 185, he is working too hard and should back off a little. On short sprints and other types of anaerobic exercise, you may go above your rate for short periods of time. This is okay; but if it doesn't go back down after an appropriate rest, this is an indication you are over-training. Your workout schedule should then be adjusted.

REST

In a sound training program, rest is as important as work. Athletes must maintain a balance between the two. One day off per week is absolutely necessary. This should be a day free of all strenuous exercise. If you are under 16, you should take two days off per week.

Over-training is more damaging than under-training. When in a slump, many athletes schedule extra training days—trying to work their way to higher levels. Often, an extended rest is the athlete's greatest need. Continuous training develops not only stale muscles but stale minds.

Swimmers and runners have done careful research on "tapering," which is the gradual decrease in training (or increase in rest) prior to major competitions. Because these sports can so accurately measure performance, their work in this area is carefully documented. Veteran coaches and athletes often have a greater respect for rest periods than their younger counterparts. We encourage respect for the wisdom of the veterans.

A good night's rest, on a consistent schedule, is important for all athletes. Added rest is needed whenever training loads are above average. Intense work-outs must be balanced with intense rest.

HYDRATION

Proper hydration is an important consideration for athletes. You can lose up to two liters of fluid per hour while exercising in a hot environment. Proper fluid replacement is vital. Don't rely on your thirst to tell you when or how much fluid to drink. This is often an unreliable source. As an active athlete, you should drink as many as ten glasses of fluid per day. Many small drinks are better than one or two large ones.

There are numerous fluid replacement drinks now on the market. Some of these are excellent; and others have little value. These drinks are most helpful *during* or shortly after *long* periods of exercise to replace fluids and carbohydrates. If you use fluid replacement drinks, select those which supply 6–8 percent carbohydrate from glucose or sucrose. Avoid the fructose based drinks. Remember that water is a great source of fluid, and has the best price!

CONCLUSION

Fitness enriches all aspects of life—nurturing the mind as well as the body. Successful skiers balance many activities and pursue many goals. They seek excellence in conditioning, nutrition, sports psychology, school, work, families, friends, and lots more. It is always a challenge to be the best person and the best athlete you can be. Work hard. Live well. And ski well.

Authors' Note: Much of the information in Part 6 has been condensed from the *Burke Mountain Academy Summer Training Manual*. It is printed here with permission from the school. BMA has earned international recognition for the high levels of fitness achieved by its student-athletes. USST members Diann Roffe Steinrotter, Julie Parisien, and Matt Grosjean (whose pictures appear in this book) are among the eleven Burke alumni who skied in the 1992 Winter Olympics. Persons interested in the academic and sports programs of BMA may contact the school at P.O. Box 78, East Burke, Vermont 05832, (802) 626-5607.

"Some of the best instruction is in children's ski school"

PART 7

PERSPECTIVES FOR INSTRUCTORS

We salute the 20,000 ski instructors in America who give their time, energy, and skill to help others learn to ski. The great majority of instructors are dedicated to the students they serve and are wonderful ambassadors for the sport. No other group does more to share with other skiers their enthusiasm for the mountains and for the many joys of skiing.

The Professional Ski Instructors of America [PSIA] have worked long and hard to achieve four goals:

1. To standardize instruction.

2. To define the fundamental elements of skiing and organize logical progressions for teaching them.

3. To maintain certification programs that earn the public's trust.

4. To give stature to the **profession** of ski teaching.

These goals have been fairly well met for beginning and novice skiers who are brought into the sport with safety and confidence. Intermediate and advanced skiers, however, have been served less well.

Ski industry surveys show that only a small percentage of intermediate or better skiers continue to take lessons; and that when they do, they're often disappointed. The failure of ski schools to help students learn carving skills and athletic skiing has serious consequences. When skiers' skills plateau at a low level, their excitement for skiing and their long term commitment to the sport declines. The industry loses customers; and the individuals miss out on the joys of expert skiing.

Many ski areas view their ski schools as cash cows that use low-paid help (instructors) to serve a captive audience (beginners). These areas have long been satisfied to serve the beginner/novice pool and accept little responsibility for helping better skiers. Thoughtful observers are now asking if this is a wise approach for the long-term health of the ski industry.

Our viewpoint is clear. We think ski schools have an opportunity, and even a responsibility, to better serve intermediate and advanced skiers. *Our interest is to help all skiers become better skiers and to reach their full potential as athletes.* We hope this book, and particularly the next five chapters, will inspire ski schools to consider new ways to serve a larger audience.

CARTOON BY VIKI FLECKENSTEIN WOODWORTH

Chapter 27

SETTING GOALS

For the past twenty years, ski schools have debated the proper balance for teaching carving and skidding skills. As we write in 1993, a majority of American schools are stuck between the forty yard lines on the Playing Field of Skiing. (See page 87). We think they should be moving toward the right end zone, and focusing more on athletic skiing.

We accept that skidding and braking skills must be taught to beginners—as one learning to drive a car must learn to use the brake. But as soon as driving skills are learned, students are taught to avoid riding the brake. Skidding turns on skis is the same as riding the brake in a car. Why have ski schools been stuck in this limited mode of skiing for so many years?

PSIA's ten-year focus on "Center-Line" skiing has set too low a standard for instructors and students alike. Defenders of "Center-Line" assert it is a concept that honors and teaches all skiing—from one end zone to the other, from skidding skills to carving skills. While they may "honor" all skiing, the truth is *they seldom teach skills that lead their students past mid-field*. In plain English, "center" means the middle, and that's the comfortable place where most ski instruction has settled.

If PSIA means "all-inclusive" when they say "Center-Line," then they need a new catchword to describe what they are doing. As a marketing tool, or a focused guide for instructors, "Center-Line" doesn't work. It *fails* to describe what PSIA says it means. It *does* describe the portion of the playing field where most instructors are teaching others, and skiing themselves.

Most instructors skid often, carve seldom, and talk constantly about "shaping turns." "Shaping turns" describes a combination of modest edging skills and rotary movements that produce a "controlled" but skidded turn.

PSIA has mastered the controlled skid. They have analyzed it, defined it, demonstrated and taught it—all with an enormous faith that it's a suitable goal for most skiers. This is the crux of PSIA's problem: ***the goal isn't high enough.*** A skidded turn is a dead end street that leaves instructors, students, and the profession of ski teaching with nowhere exciting to go. By contrast, the development of carving skills offers unlimited potential. Only a carving ski provides the foundation for dynamic, lateral movement and the freedom of athletic skiing. (See photos of Scott Tarbet, next page.)

66

Childrens' faces reveal many truths. In photos 66 and 67, Scott Tarbet defines the difference between skidding and carving. In the photo above, his downhill ski is skidding. His posture is defensive. His muscles are tense. His expression tells volumes about instability, general discomfort, and a lack of confidence for what lies ahead.

In this photo, Scott's downhill ski is carving cleanly. His stance is more erect. He's completely relaxed. He is stable, comfortable, and confident about his future. He is in control, and thoroughly enjoying it.

These remarks may oversimplify Scott's circumstances; but the fundamental truth is inescapable. A skidding ski provides an unstable platform which is ill-suited for athletic movement. A carving ski provides a secure platform that enhances athletic movement.

The carve or skid debate has been skewed for twenty years by boot and balance limitations. Carving skills are not easily learned when out of balance. If the majority of students (and their teachers) aren't properly canted, or are skiing in the back seat, they're destined to be skidders. Most students, and their instructors, have been out of balance since rigid plastic boots became common in the 1970's. ***It's time to cure this disease rather than live with it.***

After balance issues are addressed, the teaching menu can more easily be changed. When "athletic skiing" becomes the clearly established goal, the foundations for carving can be introduced at the earliest stages of instruction. PSIA needs to focus on teaching carving skills, and helping students to become athletic skiers.

The best skiers in the world are carving well and trying to carve better. Ski manufacturers are focused clearly on building skis that carve sharper turns with less effort. The designers are doing all they can to help skiers get to the right end zone. Instructors should be helping, and PSIA should be saying so loud and clear. In most cases they aren't doing so. There are, however, signs of hope.

We skied with instructors at Winter Park last winter whose motto was "Arc 'em or Park 'em." They were inspiring skiers and fun to be with on a mountain. At Deer Valley we worked with many instructors who were anxious to improve their own carving skills, and learn how to teach them. We watched a woman instructor (in another school that's rotary oriented) teach carving with great success to a class of middle-aged women executives. The instructor, a former National Team racer, said: "I teach what I know works. Most of the instructors here can't carve a turn themselves, so they don't teach the skill to others."

Thus, the debate goes on. We hope this book provides support and encouragement to those who can move PSIA toward a greater focus on athletic skiing. Some members of the D-Team are trying (see photo 68), and others in PSIA are working to move the bureaucracy in new directions. Significant change will take place only if there's strong leadership at the top, and extensive education for *all* instructors.

While awaiting this evolution, where can people go to learn athletic skiing? We suggest that most ski schools have a few instructors who are good at teaching carving skills. Many are ex-racers. Ask for them when you sign up for a lesson. Tell the supervisor: "I want an instructor who is really good at teaching carving skills." Or, "I want to learn athletic skiing." When enough students make these requests, ski schools will pay attention. When they do, they'll help their students to ski better and have more enjoyment in the sport.

Finally, we suggest that a variety of forces in the ski industry may move some ski schools to focus quickly on athletic skiing. Ask around. Good skiers will know where they are. Go there for lessons.

68

PSIA D-Team member, Greg Moss, kicks up his heels and lets loose at SnowBird. The D-Team, which represents the best instructors in PSIA, is trying to promote more athletic skiing. We wish them success, and hope this book helps.

Chapter 28

RECOGNIZING SUSPENSION PROBLEMS

Performance, at all levels of skiing, is limited by boot function. Only a small percentage of instructors are knowledgeable about the issues discussed in Part 2 of this book. To teach effectively, instructors must become experts on the relationships between suspension issues and skier performance.

The biggest fault in ski instruction today is that ski schools and ski instructors accept their students with whatever equipment they show up in—and are satisfied to teach them what they can. If students are in rental boots, or have come for just one lesson, instructors have little choice but to accept their handicaps and teach around them.

But for students who are in school for a week, or who have interest in more than one lesson, *suspension problems should be addressed first; then effective teaching can begin.*

At present, instructors have few resources to deal with boot problems. *This must change.* To be effective, ski schools must accept responsibility for meeting the equipment needs of their students. Alignment services should be offered "on site" at ski school centers. It makes no more sense to run a ski school without an attached "balance shop" than to run a car dealership that can't balance wheels and align suspensions.

This challenge requires that ski schools envision a larger role for themselves than "on the hill, follow me instruction." Whether schools provide their own balance shop, or contract the program out, the service must be provided. *"Balance first, teaching second" is as right a theory in ski school as in racing camp.* It is *efficient.* It provides the most rapid learning in the shortest time. Ski schools should be organized around the knowledge presented in Part 2 of this book.

The *balance first, teaching second* principle applies at *all* levels of ski school instruction. Whether beginner, intermediate, or expert, learning accelerates when balance is improved. In addition, the skills which can be learned are greatly expanded.

The satisfaction of students also expands. Think of students who have been "leaning in," or "in the back seat," or skiing for years with "wobbly knee syndrome." If in two lessons (one in the balance shop and one on the hill) these ingrained "compensations" or "faults" can be corrected, the students will be delighted. They'll return to ski school with respect for their instructors and renewed confidence in their learning. They will often bring friends. This approach is good for business.

PSIA should organize education programs that teach instructors to recognize suspension problems and their relationship to student performance. The principles are easily understood, and can be quickly integrated in ski school programs. This book provides a guide for all who are interested. The challenge is to push ski schools out of long established patterns and get them to accept new responsibilities and develop new programs. Those who accept this challenge will serve their customers well.

To best understand the relationship between balance problems and skiing performance, we recommend three programs to instructors. These programs are equally valuable for coaches, racers, and recreational skiers:

1. Study the "Technical Indications for Canting" chart on page 49. Put a copy in your pocket and refer to it often when watching others ski. Look for these symptoms not only in your students but wherever you observe other skiers. When riding a chairlift, every skier who passes in your view offers a study in boot function and balance. With practice, you can develop an eye for the relationships between boots, stance, and technique. Look especially at skiers' knees. What is the knee position at the moment of edge change? Inside or out? Do skiers angulate well at turn initiation? Or do they lean in with their head, and throw their hip outside? Look also at skis. Do they skid at the start of turns, showing too little edge for the position of the knee? Or are they edged too much, and too early? Study the tracks that skiers leave and relate them to the body movements you observe.

   Change your focus from studying upper-body positions and looking for "correct style" to studying *skis and knees*, and looking for efficiency. Look for good alignment and good balance. (See drawing 18 A, B, C, next page.)

   These three images correspond from left to right with the "over-canted," "ideal alignment," and "under-canted" skiers on the Technical Indications for Canting chart (page 49). They also correspond to the photos of Tina on pages 46–48. Look especially at the rear view photos on page 47. Take time now to cross reference these images with the drawings on the next page and the performance descriptions on the chart. This is *very serious business* for all ski instructors, and important knowledge for all readers.

   Which stance looks easiest to ski in? Which appears most difficult? What inefficiencies do you see in skier A and skier C?

The best perspective to study canting needs is from behind the skier, as shown in these drawings. It is easiest to study alignment by focusing on the top of the turn. The moment of edge change is the most revealing of small canting needs. Drawing 18 shows the skier when pressure is building on the ski. This part of the turn is best for studying a skier's total stance. Look first at knee positions, then at the hips, then at the head and shoulders.

18A

Over-Canted

18B

Ideal Alignment

18C

Under-Canted

DRAWINGS BY DIANE BODE

The rear view is also best for watching what the skis do at the moment of edge change and immediately after. (See photo 69 on following page.) Do the skis **skid** sideways (too little edge)? Or are they **pushed** sideways (too much edge)? It's easy to understand that a ski with too little edge will skid to the side. It's more difficult to visualize why a ski with too much edge must be pushed to the side. Consider this: If the ski comes too much on edge, and too soon, it will turn under a skier's body more sharply than knee alignment and angulation are balanced for. To control the carving power of the ski, a skier must push it far enough away from his body that he has sufficient mechanical advantage to hold it out there and "control" it. If a little over-canted, the push is subtle. If more over-canted, the push is substantial.

Only when perfectly canted, can skiers begin turns with knee and hip angulation in natural proportion, and without a lateral movement of the outside ski. To learn more, you should **experience** canting as suggested in the next paragraph.

2. Have your ski school provide "demo-skis" that have adjustable bindings with 2 degrees of cant. Ski on these with the cants thick side inside (over-canted), and thick side outside (under-canted). **The best way to understand canting is through experience.** What do you **feel** when your cants are changed, and your knees are differently aligned? Can you feel a difference in your balance and knee alignment at the

69

This is the perspective we find most useful for studying alignment needs, and a skiers ability to carve at the top of the turn. The skier here is Tommy Moe (USA), the Downhill Gold Medalist at the Lille-hammer Olympics.

moment of edge change? What happens to your stance when you have too little or too much edge in the belly of a turn? When your canting geometry is changed, what muscles are more relaxed, or more stressed? Does your stance resemble skier A when over-canted? And skier C when undercanted?

Next, adjust your boots with maximum and minimum forward lean. Change the flex. Put lifts under your heels. Change your fore/aft balance in as many ways as you can. What do you feel when you put yourself in the back seat? Or when you find perfect balance for the first time in years? Remember the 80/20 : 20/80 principle. Can you verify this with your experiments?

Only when you *experience* skiing out of balance, (and can compare this to skiing in balance) can you best understand your students' problems. Focus on how your skis react in the snow; then think carefully about the compensations you make with upper-body movements. Feel the pressures and strains on your muscles and joints. There is much to learn.

3. Tune your own suspension system until you ski in *perfect balance*. Spend a day, a week, or a month—however long it takes—but get it right. Make your boots work exactly as you want them to. Accept no compromise. Adjust your canting needs to the accuracy of 1/8 degree. When your suspension system is right, your skiing will improve; your ability to learn carving skills will be enhanced; and you'll better understand the goals your students should be reaching for.

Footnote (June 1994): We are delighted to report that we did on-snow alignment clinics with instructors from 40 major ski schools in 1994. Their reception of the ideas presented in this book was consistently enthusiastic. Many ski schools have created working relationships with bootfitters and ski shops at or near their ski areas. Some are planning to integrate bootfitting services within their ski schools over the next few years. Many are developing specific programs that train instructors to recognize technical errors caused by alignment problems. We salute the ski schools who are taking these steps.

In evaluating nearly 800 instructors, on snow, over the past year, we found: More than 80% were over-canted. Less than 10% were under-canted. Only one in ten was canted so they could ski with maximum efficiency. Those instructors who were over-canted had great difficulty carving turns. Most pushed their tails at the start of turns, used excessive hip and/or shoulder rotation, and displayed a tendency toward "banking."

The good news is: It wasn't their fault! It was their boots' fault. (See "The Blame Game," page 53.) When proper canting was provided, the ability to carve and to ski more athletically was greatly enhanced.

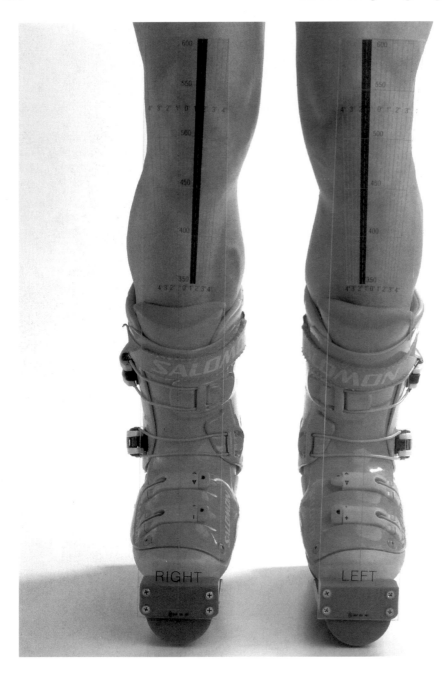

ERIK OSTLING

To make canting evaluations quicker, easier, and more accurate, The Cant Company (with design assistance from the authors) has developed "The Cant Evaluator" shown above. The round-bottom base is adjustable for all boot sizes. The location of the knee center line is shown on the lexan grid that rests against each knee. The alignment of the knee relative to the bootsole can be read directly in degrees. We recommend this evaluator to all ski shops, ski schools, race programs, and others with an interest in canting evaluations. For ordering information, see page 66.

Chapter 29

CORRECT SKIING OR ATHLETIC SKIING

Though it's a broad generalization, we think it's fair to say that ski instruction has become too mechanical. In an effort to develop consistent skiing and teaching styles, most schools have focused on defined mechanics rather than natural movement. They have honored structure and form over spontaneity and playfulness. They have forgotten that skiing is sport. The goal of skiing is not to "look pretty" or to have "good form." The goal is to have more fun.

The philosophy of learning which has long been dominant in PSIA is based on learning specific tasks in a specific order. We encourage teaching concepts, and helping students progress through experiment and exploration. This balance is admittedly difficult.

A major reason why most ski school lessons are provided to beginners and lower intermediates is that instruction is stuck in the lesson plan mode. When students have learned the basics required to get safely down the mountain, they abandon ski school and strike out on their own.

When this happens, the instructors and students are both short changed. The instructors lose business at advanced levels, and must find new beginners to teach; and the students leave school poorly equipped to continue their learning. Students who have no foundation in carving skills, are ill prepared to learn athletic skiing.

Ski schools need a new image of themselves. They need to develop programs for "college" and "graduate school" study. When good courses are offered by good instructors, advanced skiers will come back to school. Millions of intermediate and advanced skiers want to improve. At present, they don't think ski schools can help them.

We have a tongue-in-cheek description of ski instructors that draws a hearty laugh from a broad spectrum of skiers:

> *"Ski instructors remind us of golf carts. They all look alike and their maximum speed is 15 miles per hour."*

Through their laughter, the skiing public confirms their impression that most instructors are not inspiring skiers. The image they most often present is static and slow, and lacking athletic movement. This impression is widespread.

Our instructor friends laugh at the golf cart simile too. They know the shoe fits. They complain often that supervisors and area managers ask them to be models of control, precision, and decorum. *Boring* is the image they present. When in uniform, they aren't allowed to ski fast, or be playful, or "lay tracks" on the mountain. Is it any wonder that intermediate and stronger skiers aren't knocking on ski school doors and asking for lessons?

When teaching lower level classes, instructors have good reasons to be slow, safe, and programmed. At other times, they should be a "visual force" on the mountain.

Ski schools should encourage instructors to play in the bumps, to leave carving tracks under the lifts, to be spontaneous, creative, and dynamic in their skiing. Instructors need to show off their skills, and their enjoyment of skiing, as often as they can. ***In Uniform.***

If ski schools want to attract the public to high-end lessons, they must demonstrate the skills that potential students would like to learn. These are not *perfectly shaped turns* done in *perfect form* at 15 M.P.H. The public wants to dance—to learn "free skating" not "school figures." They want to learn athletic skiing. Ski schools ought to teach it.

Scot Schmidt exemplifies the kind of relaxed, natural skiing we have promoted throughout this book. Note the carved turn track behind Scott. He is never posed; and always poised. Like Karen Percy, he doesn't demonstrate a given technique or way of skiing. He skis as he walks—moving from one foot to the other. Ski instructors need to forget that people are looking at them, and just go skiing. The best thing they can show the public at large and their students in particular is instinctive, athletic movement. When they demonstrate this, they will help everyone ski in a more natural stance, with better balance, and with greater relaxation.

Chapter 30

GROWTH

There are a limited number of beginners available to teach in any given year. There are millions of intermediate and advanced skiers. If ski schools want to grow, they need new programs to serve this constituency. We suggest marketing plans titled "PSIA - Continuing Education", and "PSIA - Graduate School."

Athletic Skiers are looking for **performance.** They are spending more than ever on ski tuning services. They are purchasing more footbeds (at a cost equal to three or four days of lessons). They are paying top dollars for skis, boots, and bindings that promise a performance edge. Some are reading this book.

A ski school with an integrated balance shop, and instructors trained to use it, will attract many of these skiers. Every student in such a school would enjoy the immediate benefits of a properly tuned "suspension system"—skiing in balance and being able to learn carving skills. They could become athletic skiers. These will be happy students!

One course we recommend for an expanded ski school curriculum is FUN SCHOOL. The teachers in this program would have special parkas with "FUN SCHOOL" written in giant letters across the back. Their goal—for students at all ability levels—would be to focus on creativity and exploration, and help people to have more fun on skis. FUN SCHOOL would teach new kinds of turns; skiing backwards; doing 360's; one-ski maneuvers; games in the bumps; new ways to generate responses from their skis; and how to "play" with their edges. Developing a "syllabus" for these courses would be an exciting challenge for a whole ski school, and would stretch the imagination of many instructors. Assignment to teach these classes would be a "plum" in daily line-ups.

Most important, the FUN SCHOOL instructors would have an impact on the spirit of their mountain. They would project images of playfulness, spontaneity, and imagination that ski schools need. If these qualities spilled over into all parts of a ski school's work, that would be a plus for students and instructors alike. A FUN SCHOOL program would attract a great many intermediate and advanced skiers who haven't taken lessons for years.

There's an axiom in education that learning becomes more structured and less successful with each year of schooling. In kindergarten and the lower grades, students have unstructured seating, free "play-time," and learning is based on discovery and experimentation. Children are given tools to play with and *guided freedom* to explore. In high school, the desks are placed in neat rows and learning becomes more linear. Wise educators deplore this occurrence.

There is a parallel in teaching skiing. Some of the best instruction is in children's ski school. Quick, effective, and unstructured learning goes on there. Some of the principles that are well developed for teaching children could be effective with adults. A FUN SCHOOL could explore these opportunities.

In closing this chapter, we must stress that our goal is not to re-invent ski schools, but to help them grow. We are hopeful that balance services will expand, that carving skills will be better taught, that there will be a greater emphasis on athletic skiing, and a new curriculum for better skiers. These programs could enhance the joys of skiing for many people who are currently skipping school.

Each of these growth areas offers new opportunities for professional ski teachers. At present, instructors are grossly underpaid for the work they do. Most teach more for love than for money—not by choice, but because there's little financial reward as ski schools are structured. For rookies, the pay with skiing benefits may be appropriate. For experienced instructors who are dedicated, long-term teachers, higher rewards are due. High-end services require better teachers with better training. If they were appropriately paid by ski school management, more good men and women could justify long-term commitments to teaching skiing. They could, indeed, become "professional." With their leadership, ski schools could grow, ski areas could prosper, and the whole ski industry would be stronger.

When skiers are more successful, they have more enjoyment in the sport. They ski more days, buy better equipment, and purchase condos in the mountains. The ski industry laments the number of skiers who "drop out" each year. We suggest working hard to help intermediate skiers become experts. Those who learn to dance go skiing more often than those who continue to slip and slide.

Chapter 31

CERTIFICATION, STANDARDIZATION, AND FREEDOM

In a broad variety of human endeavors, certification programs stifle imagination, creativity, and change. This is certainly true in education; and it's true in PSIA.

The golf-cart syndrome is a direct outgrowth of PSIA's focus on "correct" ways to ski, "correct" ways to demonstrate, and "correct" ways to teach. In their efforts to standardize instruction, they have stifled their instructors. By too carefully defining demonstration maneuvers, they have shackled the demonstrators. Consistency has been gained. But freedom, innovation, and athleticism have been lost.

Please consider: At a major league baseball game, you see eighteen or more batters. Each one holds the bat differently, and takes a different stance. Some hold the bat high, some low. Some vertical, and some horizontal. They stand closed or open or square, and their feet may be 3 inches or 30 apart. Every body works in a different way. Each athlete must find the stance and swing that works best for him. Similarly, the golf swing of Jack Nicklaus is nothing like that of Arnold Palmer. But both are winners.

Luckily, in baseball, only the objective batting average counts; and in golf, the number of strokes. But for instructor certification, close adherence to defined norms is required. Examiners look for performance in too narrow a range. Their view of "correct" is too limited. They nitpick at small details, and show too little respect for creative teaching and skiing.

We think it's more important for instructors to demonstrate spontaneity, playfulness, and imagination than "perfect turns." Look at children's ski school. Instructors ski without poles, do goofy things with their hands and heads, play games of fox and hound. They should teach adult beginners the same way. Certification exams should give as much credit to playful instructors as to "perfect" ones.

Every body functions best and balances best in a slightly different way. Ski racers from the same team show far more individuality in their styles than instructors from the same school. What finally counts in skiing is the track one leaves in the snow. Who can best make his skis go where he wants them to go and respond on command? Who is the most energetic and athletic. Skiing is a dynamic sport. A skier's versatility is more important than adherence to a norm.

Instructors must be encouraged to be explorers. Performance and freedom should be the goals of skiing, not perfection and control. It's the 90's—the age of the athletic skier. It's time to get off the brake and onto the accelerator. Let's learn to exploit the energy in our bodies and our skis. It's time to have more fun on skis, and to pin a medal on those instructors who can show us how.

Who wants to drive golf carts when sports cars are available? Or ride tricycles when mountain bikes are close at hand?

"Fundamentals win races at all levels of skiing."

PART 8

PERSPECTIVES FOR RACERS
(AND OTHER PERFORMANCE SKIERS)

Nearly all the information presented in this book is directly applicable to racing. For developing racers, the fundamentals of carving turns and good balance are most important. *Fundamentals win races at all levels of skiing*. The information on boot-fitting and skeletal alignment in Part 2 is especially important for competitors.

Ski racing demands athletic performance, not a specific technique. Each athlete develops a style, or patterns of movement, that are most efficient for his or her body. It is difficult, therefore, to play "coach" to all ski racers from in front of a word processor.

What help can we be to a broad spectrum of racers and other performance skiers who are looking for an edge? ***We can serve best by helping athletes learn to help themselves.**** In the next few chapters, we'll share insights gained over many years. We hope our points of view help younger athletes to reach their goals.

Readers with a special interest in racing are urged to read the various publications of the U.S. Ski Team and the U.S. Ski Coaches Association. The Journal of the USSCA, *The American Ski Coach*, has become an increasingly valuable resource in recent years. The *USST Alpine Training Manual* is a rich resource for information on racing technique, line, tactics, and training strategies.*

*USSCA/USST, P.O. Box 100, Park City, UT 84060. (801) 649-9090.

Chapter 32

THE SCIENTIFIC ATHLETE

Ski races are won, or lost, by 1/100 of a second. At slalom speeds that is 3 inches. At giant slalom speed, 8 inches.

Ski racing demands the greatest attention to details in equipment preparation. Coaches and racers must stop worrying about athletes becoming "too equipment conscious". In the 1990's athletes must be "equipment smart" or pay serious penalties on the race hill.

The dominant racers from Jean Claude Killy to the present have been extremely careful and knowledgeable about their equipment. Killy spent an extraordinary amount of time perfecting the Dynamic skis he raced on. He had not only an equipment advantage but a psychological advantage as well.

Stenmark and the Mahres, who dominated skiing in the late 70's and early 80's, were deeply involved in the design of their equipment. Marc Girardelli fits in the same mold today. He exhibits *perfect* balance in his skiing. All of these champions have worked with great care on their boots, their skis, and suspension alignments. The same is true of the leaders on the pro tour. Ove Nygren began canting his boots when he was thirteen. His dad taught him how. He insists, today, that precise canting is imperative for success at the top levels of skiing.

Far from being distracted by their attention to equipment, these athletes' lives and careers have been enriched and stimulated by their interest in it. This is the attitude coaches and racers should work to create.

Where do the most intelligent racers come from? Sometime in their youth they became curious. They started thinking, exploring, experimenting. They sought out the best coaches they worked with, picked their brains for all the knowledge they could get, and went on to learn more on their own. This is the path young racers should follow.

At Junior and Development levels, the wisest athletes form good relationships with their ski and boot companies as well as their coaches. They learn whatever their coaches and service personnel can teach them. They ask questions, confirm answers, then go another step with their own research. They are always curious, always learning. If you learn enough at ages twelve to twenty, you have a better chance to promote your interests when you get to the National Team. At every level of racing, ***you need a knowledge base so strong you can trust your own judgement.***

Junior racers have many opportunities to experiment with equipment. They can borrow from friends — exploring different brands of skis and skis with different flexes. Because they are home rather than travelling, they have the time, and the tools in their own shop, to experiment in ways less available to racers on the circuit. Young racers can experiment with canting and fore/aft balance. These experiments keep them focused on how their skis are working in the snow, and how efficiently they can ski. Every experiment helps to build a knowledge base.

We encourage all racers to be consistently curious about skis and boots in general, and about their own skis and boots in particular. Don't be "equipment freaks"; but do be inquisitive and intelligent, and always learning.

Many coaches will complain this approach confuses an athlete —that young skiers are better served to take whatever equipment they have and just go skiing. This is a correct approach for some days and some parts of a season; but, on other days, it insults the athlete's intelligence. Ignorance is seldom a virtue, or a long-term aid to success. Youth is a time for learning. A wise coach encourages the growth of curiosity in every child.

Even with the best of all manufacturers and service personnel, racers must make final equipment choices. The manufacturer may produce a dozen superior skis. The racer must choose the best of them. The manufacturer may produce a wonderful boot. The racer has to fine tune it. The most successful racers work as a team with their coaches and servicemen.

The bottom line is that young racers, both boys and girls, should be *fascinated* by ski equipment. They should make learning all they can about skis and boots and bindings a priority in their programs. Not only does this assure better results at every stage of their careers; it may land them good jobs in the ski industry when racing days are over.

Chapter 33

SUSPENSION SYSTEMS FOR RACING

Charly Kahr, the great Austrian downhill coach of the Klammer era, said:

> "If your boots are right, you gain two seconds.
> If your wax is right, you gain two tenths.
> If your uniform is right, you gain two hundredths."

In all that we have written about boots, it is clear they are the most critical link in the performance equation. Review Part 2, and *be certain* you have gained every possible advantage. This includes:

1. Selection of the best available boot model for *your* foot, *your* technique, and *your* application.
2. Proper fitting of an orthotic.
3. Proper adjustment of the boot for flex, cuff alignment, ramp angle, forward lean, etc.
4. Proper canting.

Let's consider the special attention racers must give to these issues.

SELECTION OF THE BEST AVAILABLE BOOT

There are many challenges here, and meeting them is difficult. Curiosity, ingenuity, and time are required. We are not aware of any boot demo programs similar to the extensive ski programs now available. What is to be done?

First, understand your task. From ten or more appropriate models, you must find the *best one* for your foot and your skiing demands. ***The difference in performance from one boot to another is much larger than most people realize.***

As a part of the research for this book, Warren Witherell skied on seven different boots in 1993. All were properly fitted and foamed. Substantial modifications were made to optimize flex and fore/aft balance. Custom orthotics were properly interfaced. Two boots were impossible to ski well in. Three were tolerable, but clearly limited performance. One pair was good. And one pair was extraordinary.

The best boots did not fit perfectly out of the box. They required two weeks of careful, professional adjustment. A shoemaker moved the tongue and closure straps on the liner. The shells were expanded to accommodate foot abnormalities. Orthotics were built, integrated to the boot, and fine tuned. Cuff, forward lean, and ramp angle were set. Initial canting needs were met with sole grinding; and final canting was done with a few strips of tape under the bindings. Warren has difficult feet; but so do most other people. Every step in this process contributed to more perfect boot function. The design of the boot was never changed. It was simply custom fitted.

It is surely difficult for most people—racers or recreational skiers—to try a variety of boots on snow. We tell Warren's story because it provides a symbol of the rewards available for finding the *best possible* boot, and doing everything necessary to make it fit perfectly. What can average consumers, who are unable to test boots on snow, do to improve their chances of getting the best possible boots?

A) Try on as many boots as you can. Visit more than one boot shop, and don't accept the first recommendation of the salesman. Make lots of time (days not hours) available for the selection process. Don't be hurried.

B) When trying on boots, some clearly will not fit your foot. Some will feel too stiff or too soft. (Remember they are stiffer when cold.) Some will require excessive canting adjustment. Eliminate the misfits. Then with the best two or three options, spend a *lot* of time in them. Walk around a boot shop for two hours. Settle in. If you buy them, you'll ski in them for six to eight hours at a time. Spend time with the boots *on edge*. Lean against the wall, a chair, a counter. On a carpet, put skis on so you can leverage forward and back. Adjust the flex, cuffs, and ramp angle as well as you can without owning the boots. Simulate skiing in as many ways as you can. Accept no compromise. The right boot gives you two seconds. Search 'til you find it.

C) Don't choose a boot because your favorite World Cup skier uses it, or your best friend loves it, or you can get a discount on it, or it's the product your favorite ski shop is pushing this year. Your boots are the most important piece of equipment you have. Take your time. Buy *your* boot, not someone else's.

D) Don't purchase a "new model" from a manufacturer for whom you have brand loyalty without first testing against all other boots available, including your present ones. We salute brand loyalty, especially when companies have provided good service and support in the past. But, if there is a better boot, you must choose it. Sometimes new models are better than old ones. Just as often they're not.

Many World Cup racers use boots that are three to five years old, or models that are even older, and sometimes out of production. Despite pressure from sponsors to use and promote new models, these racers know that the older boots *work best for them*. Some use the same shells for many seasons and replace the liners as needed. Others wear out the shells first, and re-use the liners. New is not always better. The *only* thing that counts is boot *function*. How well does the boot work on *your* foot and for *your* specific need?

If you find a pair of boots you really love—that provide exceptional performance and comfort—*never* give them up for something new unless the new product is clearly better. Treasure a great pair of boots, and take the best possible care of them. Always wear *Cat-Tracks* to protect the soles. Never assume you can get another, better pair when new models are available.

PROPER FITTING OF AN ORTHOTIC

Review Chapter 4 on orthotics and footbeds. There is a huge gap in this area of boot-fitting between what is ideal and what is practical. There are few resources for acquiring really good orthotics that are properly interfaced with your boots. Most recreational skiers and mid-level racers have to settle for a good footbed. But most top level racers, or skiers at any level who want to ski as well as possible, must get a true orthotic. A good orthotic allows a skier to transmit energy to his skis with optimum power and precision. There is a great need for new research, new products, and expanded services in this area of performance enhancement.

We are aware that many skiers have tried orthotics and been unhappy with them. In many cases these were built by orthotists who have little experience with ski boots and the special needs of skiers. This includes the need for 2–6 degrees of loose adaption in the boot, and proper interfacing of the orthotic with each specific boot. When done properly, orthotics can help the performance of 90% of all skiers. The ski industry is just beginning to address these issues.

PROPER ADJUSTMENT OF ALL BOOT FUNCTIONS

Review Chapters 5 and 6. For skiers with high performance goals, the smallest changes in flex, ramp angle, shaft alignment, etc., are significant. Fore/aft balance, for instance, can be altered in five ways: by raising the heel in the orthotic; by changing the ramp angle; by changing forward lean in the cuff; by altering the flex of the boot (which can be done a variety of ways); and by raising or lowering the heel outside the boot. *Perfect fore/aft balance is essential for a racer*. All of the above adjustments work in subtly different ways. Explore all options, and accept no compromise. Don't let the false security of the "phantom foot" lure you into accepting less than a perfectly balanced stance.

CANTING

Review Chapter 7. The basic details are outlined there. Racers seeking advantages that are measured by hundredths of a second, must be very precise in finding their optimum leg alignment. All racers (and other performance skiers) should be sensitive to canting adjustments as small as 1/4 degree. Those with the greatest sensitivity and precision can feel changes as small as 1/8 degree which is 5/1000 of an inch or one strip of Scotch Decorate & Repair Tape. Only trial and error can find the optimum stance for each skier. It may be slightly different for Slalom than for GS, Super G, or Downhill.

Skeptics say that coaches and racers who try to be this precise are techno-geeks. "Real athletes," they say, "just go skiing. They adapt. They don't have to be so scientific." This point of view is absolutely unacceptable in competitive sport in the 1990's. Good athletes *can* adapt, and they *can* ski well; but **without perfect alignment, they can never ski to their full potential.**

Some price must always be paid for adaptation. Balance, quickness, agility, power, and efficiency all suffer to some degree. *Perfect alignment*, and the balance it provides, must be our goal.

Many racers will ask: "Do I really have to worry about all this equipment stuff? Can't I just be an athlete and compete with my strength, technique, and tactics?" We respect the instincts that prompt these questions. Racers who have worked hard in physical training, and have run ten thousand gates, want to compete as athletes not boot mechanics. They want to look their competitors in the eye and say "Let's get it on. Let's see who has speed today? My athletic ability against yours."

We applaud this instinct. It's all you need if wrestling or swimming is your sport. In skiing, however, it's not enough. Skiing is a high-tech, equipment-dependent sport. Take it or leave it; you buy into that when you choose to be a ski racer. Our interest is to help you understand the relationships between equipment and performance and use them to your advantage.

Chapter 34

PRECISION ALIGNMENT

Measurement of canting needs, as described in Chapter 8, will place an athlete within one degree of optimum alignment. The fine tuning after that must be done by trial and error. Racers must experiment with fine canting adjustment by putting tape on their bindings as shown in photo 71.

Some binding companies and most ski shops will protest that this is unsafe and unwise. In public, they protect themselves from litigation. In private, they admit it works. The fact is that up to 1 degree of tape doesn't significantly alter binding function. Hundreds of racers have experimented with tape on their bindings for twenty years. Walking on pavement and scarring your bootsoles has a greater effect on binding release.

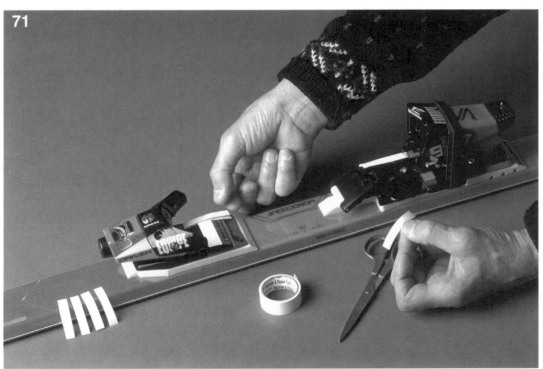

71

Some of the best racers on the Pro Tour change their canting between runs by putting tape on top of their bindings. They do this to adjust for the increasingly deep ruts they encounter on the same course. Subtle changes in canting (they under-cant more as the ruts deepen) help them to ski faster.

We don't recommend skiing all winter with tape on your bindings; but we do insist it's perfectly safe for limited testing and experimentation. Just limit your use of tape to 1 degree, or a thickness of 1 millimeter. (At a 3/8 inch width, this is eight strips of D&R Tape.)

When you find that (X) strips of tape is about right, put that amount **under** your bindings, as in photo 72, and continue to experiment with one or two strips on top for final evaluations. Under the bindings, mount the tape 3/4 inch wide. Because the tape is wider, this requires only six strips of D&R tape per degree. If you sand or plane your boot soles, go back to tape research afterward. It's hard to know *exactly* how much you plane off.

ERIK OSTLING

Experiment until you find what is most efficient. Find the skeletal alignment that permits you to edge and pressure your skis with the greatest precision. Find the alignment that provides the greatest relaxation in your skiing, and the most natural angulation.

When you find the canting geometry that works best for you, record it carefully. Use the *Cant Evaluation Form* on page 55, or the *Canting Profile* chart shown opposite. USST Coach, Bruce Lingelbach, developed this chart for tracking the athletes he works with. If you have a record of your measurements, you can refer back to them when your boots break down or you change to a new pair. We encourage racers and other skiers to maintain permanent records of their alignment position. Suspension system checks should be made at least monthly. We recommend weekly for serious racers. The entire process takes only five minutes. When you become "canting aware," you should be able to *feel* changes in your skiing as small as 1/4 degree. The most sensitive skiers can feel 1/8 of a degree (which is one strip of tape). Developing this level of awareness should be the goal of all racers.

SUSPENSION SYSTEMS CHANGE OVER TIME

For racers at all levels, mid-season changes in boot geometry have a significant affect on performance. Skiers' suspension systems work their way out of alignment just as cars' do. Boots break in and break down with each day of use. Often canting geometry changes as this happens. These changes are gradual and subtle, and are seldom recognized by racers and coaches. *They see the technical mistakes which develop, but fail to see that alignment is the cause.*

Often skiers have good results early in a season, then suffer a gradual decline. Playing the "blame game," they look everywhere in their technical skiing for solutions. Their "mistakes" are easy to identify but hard to correct.

When mature racers develop technical errors such as leaning in with the head, becoming less disciplined with hand and arm movements, or getting caught in the back seat — they are almost always compensating for balance problems that begin in the boot. Good racers who angulate well in December, but "lean in" in February, haven't forgotten how to ski. They haven't consciously changed their technique. Their bodies have made gradual adaptations and compensations as their boot geometry has changed. When the boots are fixed, upper body "errors" correct immediately.

Many racers slide from five to twenty places on the World Cup or other race series because of subtle changes in canting need. Boot breakdown is not the only factor that can change canting geometry in mid-season. The human body is a constantly changing dynamic system. A serious fall can alter a skier's alignment—requiring a physical therapist, chiropractor, or orthopedic specialist to provide realignment. Leg alignment can also be affected by changes in an athlete's flexibility or strength. As skiers move from strength and flexibility levels achieved at the end of fall training to the levels they sustain in mid-winter, their canting geometry may change as much as a degree. This can mean two or more seconds per race, and DNF's as well. Skier suspension systems, like Indy Race Cars, must be constantly kept in tune.

Many racers *are* successful who pay no attention to canting. If you ask some of the World Cup leaders what they do about canting, they shrug their shoulders and say: "I

Canting Profile

Name:

Date:

	Brand	Model	Size	Discipline	Flex
Boots:					

Leg Characteristics:

Current Setup (cuffs, sole grind, etc.)

Width of stance:

Plumb line measurement

Right boot toe		Left boot toe	

Modifications:

New plumb line measurement

Right boot toe		Left boot toe	

Comments:

CHART DESIGN BY BRUCE LINGELBACH, USST

don't worry about that. I just ski." If this is their attitude, *and they are winning*, we assure you their boot servicemen are very savvy, or they were born with legs that provide proper alignment in the boots they're using. These are the lucky athletes. Many others are not so lucky.

For every great champion who has won without canting, there have been four other skiers **with equal athletic ability** who have failed because their canting needs were never met. Some were washed out of programs at 14, some at 18, and others at 22. Countries with a huge talent pool may be able to afford such losses as a nation; but still we mourn for the individual racers whose dreams weren't realized for lack of knowledge from their coaches. The coaches should be ashamed.

There are, without question, racers now struggling at Europa Cup and Nor-Am races whose natural talents are sufficient to ski on the World Cup, and perhaps to be winners there. These racers are consistently handicapped by alignment failures. The same scenario is repeated at every level of racing, where many skiers perform well below their potential because their boots don't work well enough, or the alignment of their legs is inefficient.

The tragedy is that these racers, and their coaches, blame their failures on a lack of talent. Nowhere in skiing is the "blame game" more evident than in racing.

Until the time when all coaches understand and attend to the canting needs of their athletes, we encourage racers to take responsibility for their own suspension systems. Remember that even the best trained coach can't prescribe the final 1/2 or 1/4 degree of canting that is best for any skier. No coach or testing device can measure the subtlest feelings of edge change and skeletal alignment that a good skier can feel.

All of the above remarks apply equally to alignment and boot function on the fore/aft plane. Perfect fore/aft balance is required for optimum racing performance. There are *many* athletes at all levels of racing who are out of balance to the rear. This is especially true of women.

One U.S. Ski Team coach told us that ***"90 percent of all the skiers at the 1993 U.S. National Championships were in the back seat."*** Some of these racers may have the athletic potential to compete well on the world cup circuit. It's hard to get there from the back seat.

CHOOSING ROLE MODELS

We have to be careful here; but we'd like to make a point. What you see at the National Championships in any given year may not be the most efficient skiing. There are fads that come and go; and some athletes do well despite their handicaps. The strongest and most athletic are more able to compensate for alignment errors than racers who are less strong and less athletic.

If young racers go home from the Nationals with an image of a stance that some of the best racers in the country are using, they may assume the back seat is fast and something they should copy. They lack the perspective of the ski team coach who has been watching the best in the world. What he sees is that consistent winners on the World Cup are perfectly centered over their skis.

Our perspective, based on thirty years of film study, is that the *consistent winners* are better balanced and skiing with greater efficiency than the racers who are 4th and 8th and 15th, etc. We have crystal clear memories of the best runs by Killy, Thoeni, Stenmark, the Mahres, Girardelli, and Tomba—the best of all time on their very best days. These skiers were in exquisite balance—incredibly light on their feet, quick, agile, relaxed, efficient. These images stand out in our minds as uniquely different from those who were a few seconds behind.

Extraordinary athletes win some races despite alignment handicaps. *Consistent winners* are those who have perfect alignment and perfect balance. If you are looking for role models, choose only the very best of the consistent winners.

BEWARE WHEN CHANGING BOOTS

Racers often make substantial moves in World Cup Standings when they change boots. Some move up. Others move down. Some change brands (for commercial endorsement reasons) and fail to ski as well as in older models. Others change to new models (again for commercial reasons) and fail to ski as well. We could provide a long list of racers whose careers have been hindered by boot changes. There are, of course, others whose performances improve.

Whenever a change in boots is made, even to a new pair of the same model, it's imperative that careful attention be given to all alignment needs. Remember, too, that new boots are especially likely to break down in the first weeks of use. *It's not enough to get your alignment right in November and assume it will be right all winter.*

A special warning is needed for racers going to important training camps with new boots. We have seen countless Junior racers who skied well for a season, earned an invitation to a National Camp, went in June or October with a new pair of boots, and skied horribly.

Unless you are very, very lucky, it takes a long time to *perfectly* "dial in" a new pair of boots. It takes many days, and often weeks to get all aspects of a boot working perfectly. This can't be done at a seven or ten day camp with important time trials. Go to training camps in old boots you know you can ski well in. Experiment with new boots in relaxed settings where immediate performance is not required.

TEAMWORK

Racers should ask their coaches and reps to work with them as a team to achieve perfect balance in their boots. The racer must take the lead and be team captain. This may seem difficult for younger racers, but it must be done. Racers should call their coaches and servicemen together and say: "I need you to work together and help me have the best suspension system possible." The coach has technical knowledge and goals. The servicemen have tools, equipment, and boot-specific expertise. The racer senses his own balance, efficiency, and performance. The knowledge and skill of all three must be combined.

BEVELLING SKI BASES

Many racers, recreational skiers, and ski tuning shops advocate bevelling ski bases. They claim it "makes skiing easier." Some swear by 1 degree of bevel; others argue for 2. What's the "advantage"?

We have explored this subject with great care. With *very few* exceptions, ski manufacturers tell us their skis perform best when the bases are flat—*perfectly flat* with the steel edge recessed .001–.002 of an inch. Top racers, *who we know are perfectly canted*, assure us their skis work best when flat. One says simply: "If the bases are bevelled, the skis make surf turns."

We are convinced that ***most skiers who advocate bevelling their bases are in fact over-canted.*** It helps your perspective to remember that a majority of all skiers are over-canted in today's boots. Because their boots force their knees out, they get too much edge from their skis. Canting is simple geometry. One degree of bevel under the ski base is the same as 1 degree under the bootsole. Bevelling the ski base does help their stance; and it eases some problems of over-edging. It also hinders ski performance. That's a net loss. *The ski base is not the best place to cant.*

If you are an advocate of bevelling ski bases, we suggest you check your canting needs. Return to Part 2.

EXPERIMENT IN RELAXED SETTINGS

Boot-fitting experiments and studies of canting should be done at times of the year when important races are not imminent.

The best time is in the late spring. Summer Camps are useful. Final tuning should be checked in the first weeks on snow each winter, ***then carefully monitored throughout the season.***

Spring is the best time to borrow friends' boots, to experiment with significant changes in fore/aft balance and the effects of canting. Use video if you can. Sometimes things show up on video that you miss in real-time skiing.

Because boots are so critical a part of racing equipment, we'd like to see demo programs developed that would allow racers to experiment with various boots on snow. Within a given race program, boot-swapping days could be set up in late March. It is often possible to borrow only shells, and use your own liners. Don't expect a perfect fit; but do appreciate that many liners work well in other shells. Some skiers switch liners permanently using one brand of boot and another liner.

Switching boots allows a skier to experience the significant differences in stance, flex, power, and performance of other designs. Whether or not you like the boots you try, you always learn; you gain a better understanding of how boots work.

At the USST level—where performance is so important—we'd like to see the boot manufacturers in the team pool organize a testing camp and let all the athletes experiment. The racers should be free to switch suppliers. This would require humility and courage from the manufacturers. Some would lose. Some would gain. Some would swap. But in the end, every racer would have the best possible boots, and the team would have the best performance.

This is a radical idea in an age of contracts, agents, and commercialism. It is, however, a right idea. Choosing footwear for ski racing is not the same as for basketball. The measurable performance difference between two brands of sneakers is minimal. Between two brands of ski boots it's substantial. Should a racer switch for a gain of one second per run? One-tenth? One-hundredth? Each athlete must make his or her choice. We encourage knowing what the choices are.

Experimenting with different boots should be as integral a part of preparing a ski racer for optimum performance as experimenting with tires on race cars. Find what works best, then use them.

CANTING EXPERIMENTS

Canting experiments should be done by all racers in the same manner as described for instructors in Chapter 28, pages 169–170. A few days in the spring or fall should be set aside to carefully study canting. People are ignorant of canting because they haven't studied it. They've done no research. They have no experience. ***Canting and other suspension issues are really simple. There is no mystery . . . only unfamiliarity.***

To learn, you must experiment with using too much edge and too little. Learn what feelings you get, what technical adjustments you must make, what different responses you get from your skis. This knowledge is valuable just to better understand skiing in general and your strengths and weaknesses in particular. After doing this research, you'll be more able to identify changes in your skiing that are caused by canting needs.

A few days of this kind of learning will contribute more to your long term racing success than the same days spent beating up and down a course (as you will do a hundred other days). If you need cants or other alignment adjustment, you are practicing mistakes while training. Get your suspension right first. Then practice skiing with a more efficient technique.

It is useful to ask how many hours an average Junior racer spends sharpening edges in a normal season. An hour a day is common for serious athletes. Multiply that by a hundred days. Then ask how many hours are spent exploring canting and other suspension issues. For most racers, the answer will vary from zero to two. Does this make sense? A perfect suspension system will contribute far more to racing success than seven days of sharper edges or better wax. ***The suspension system — once you get it right — improves every turn you make all winter, in training and in racing.***

Charly Kahr had it right: "The boots give you two seconds. The wax two-tenths." Think about it.

POSTSCRIPT, FROM AN ENGLISH TEACHER.

In John Steinbeck's novel, *The Pearl*, there's a poignant scene where a peasant family takes their sick baby to an unscrupulous doctor. Wisely, they do not trust the doctor; but they are forced ***"to weigh their certain ignorance against the doctor's possible knowledge."***

Racers, who are out of balance and playing the blame game, are handicapped by their *certain ignorance*, and are dependent on the *possible knowledge* of their coaches. In truth, few coaches are well trained to recognize or correct alignment problems. We have seen many, many athletes fail to reach their goals in skiing—not because they lacked talent, but because they lacked knowledge. This is true at all levels of skiing including the World Cup.

In skiing, as in life, knowledge is power. Only the curious and diligent acquire it.

Chapter 35

THREE WAYS TO LEARN

There are many ways to learn good race technique. The most important are: by watching others; by experiment and exploration; and by acquiring understanding from coaches, articles, and books.

WATCH OTHERS

There are enough World Cup and professional races on television now that racers have many opportunities to copy the best skiers in the world. Take advantage of this opportunity via live TV and video tape. The best racers can serve as an inspiration and as technical models for skiers with many fewer skills. Just remember that both technique and tactics are strength dependent.

It's important that you do *not* try to copy another racers style. All bodies work differently. If you try too closely to imitate your favorite World Cup racer (or another good skier with whom you train) you may be forcing yourself into a style that's not natural for your body build and your coordination. You must especially remember that World Cup racers are incredibly strong. They can do things that are impossible for teenagers and Masters racers to copy.

You can, however, learn a great deal about basic stance, and about edging and pressuring skills. While dynamic movement may catch your eye at first, look carefully for the discipline, economy of motion, and consistent balance the best racers exhibit. Emulate their rhythm and grace as much as their aggressive movement.

When studying films or watching video, *start by watching skis!* See how they behave in the snow. How are they edged at the start of a turn? When is pressure applied? When is pressure distribution forward, neutral, or aft? When do the edges release and re-engage in cross-under movements? Focus for entire runs on a racers knees, or use of hip angulation, or use of the hands and arms.

On video tape, you can review good runs in slow motion or stop-action. When studying line, be sure to watch *only a racer's skis* in some runs. What line does a racer choose? How close to each gate does he run his skis, in fall line gates and in sharper turns? Then focus on the racer's center of mass. See how the CM line differs from the path of the skis. How does the racer harness the force of gravity when the CM and ski paths diverge?

For the best racers, the upper body provides balance while the lower body does most of the technical and athletic work. Study hip position on the fore/aft plane. When do the best racers have their CM forward of their boots, centered over, or behind their boots?

Whenever you study film, focus on the *best* racers when they have their *best* runs. The top five skiers in each discipline are clearly superior to the next five. Girardelli's balance and stance is better than those of the racers he consistently beats. For each race, pick the winner and find out what he or she has done better than anyone else. Learn from many; but focus intently on the best.

Good ski racers, like good athletes in all sports, must always be learning more than their coaches teach them. Your own curiosity, thoughtfulness, intelligence, and imagination must be your prime teachers. Be alert. Don't just *watch* other skiers. *Study* them. *Think* about what you observe. Work hard to be more and more observant as your career progresses. As your knowledge base grows, you have more tools with which to learn, and to improve your skiing.

Never forget that imagination is a powerful resource for the active learner. The challenge for all great coaches and athletes is to progress beyond the knowledge that's already public. New combinations of thought and understanding are always possible. Be an innovator, an inventer, an original thinker. You may discover some things that work only for you, and others that are more widely applicable. There's as much pleasure in the work of the mind as the work of the body. When skiing, engage both. The smartest athlete wins many contests.

LEARN BY EXPERIMENT AND EXPLORATION

We have written many times in this book of the need for skiers to be creative, spontaneous, imaginative, and playful. This applies as well to racers as to the public. Trial and error is a great teacher. The smartest racers are always doing "original research" with both their equipment and technique.

Racers have an extraordinary need to be disciplined, precise, and consistent. But, they must not become robots. Especially in America, racers spend too much time running gates, and too little time free skiing on the mountain. If you are a good enough skier, running gates is easy. Wherever the poles are set, you can ski. A great all-around skier is more adaptable and more instinctive than those who train too often in the gates.

One reason the Europeans have dominated racing over the past twenty years is that they are simply better mountain skiers. Racing skills are a specific adaptation of skiing skills. Racing skills don't hold up under pressure without a strong foundation of all-terrain skiing skills. The all-terrain skier has an edge in balance, adaptability, and ingenuity. When you free ski, don't just make arcing turns on groomed boulevards. Ski runs with the most varied and challenging terrain. Ski rolls, side hills, bump fields, and gullies. Racers who lack this background can't expect to do well on courses with difficult terrain.

To learn by experiment, you must never be afraid to fall. There are times in serious training and in competition when you must be entirely disciplined. Other times, in training, you should ski intentionally outside your comfort zone. If you practice only what you know, you learn but slowly. If you keep exploring for new possibilities, your body discovers and learns more quickly.

LEARN FROM COACHES, ARTICLES, AND BOOKS

Some athletes learn best by watching others. Some by experimenting themselves. Others by reading and thinking. Regardless of how you learn best, we urge you to become intellectual learners as well. Ideas and concepts are important. The more you know, the more weapons you have as an athlete. We have known many racers who skied with the best in the world though they were not the most physically gifted. They won more with brainpower than athletic talent.

Many young racers learn only what their coaches teach them. They listen when spoken to, but fail to seek information. We urge you to be inquisitive. Ask questions of coaches, service personnel, manufacturers, and other racers. Don't forget that sometimes "old folks" know more than young folks. Many young people are hesitant to communicate *openly and on even ground* with adults. The wisest adults enjoy young people who are curious and anxious to learn. Good coaches are usually good teachers. They enjoy inquisitive pupils.

Alpine racing is one of the most technical and scientific of all modern sports — both in body movement and equipment design. There is a great deal still to be learned. In this book, we have tried to collect the most pertinent information available in 1993. *We are painfully aware of how little we know. There is much to be learned next year and every year for a long time to come.* Ski coaching is only at a middle stage of development when compared to numerous other sports. Thus, there are many opportunities for intelligent skiers to prevail over more physically gifted ones.

"The ten qualities of an athletic skier that were outlined in Chapter 2 provide the foundations for good race technique."

PART 9

TECHNIQUES FOR RACING AND ADVANCED ATHLETIC SKIING

We have stressed throughout this book that athletic skiers—at all levels of recreational skiing—should look to racers for technical role models. Now we look from the racers' point of view and ask "What should our goals be? What are the secrets of racing technique?" The obvious answer is: They are the same as for all athletic skiing. The ten qualities of an athletic skier that were outlined in Chapter 2 provide the foundations for good race technique.

Good racing is good skiing. There are no secret techniques. There is no Austrian or French or Norwegian turn that needs to be learned. The best racers are those who have mastered the fundamentals stressed throughout this book. For the particular demands of racing, we can focus on special applications of these fundamentals, applying them to considerations of speed and line.

There is no one technique for all. Each athlete must find his or her unique way. But one cannot, in the guise of individuality, run counter to the laws of physics. Fundamentals are basic. Each athlete must develop a style and technique that best utilizes the common laws of physics.

In the two chapters that follow, we'll draw attention to those principles that demand the greatest attention from racers.

Chapter 36

FIVE FOUNDATIONS

The five most important foundations for modern racing technique are:

1. Good Balance
2. Economy of Motion
3. The Mastery of Carving Skills
4. The Development of Athletic Movement
5. The Utilization of Gravity

GOOD BALANCE

Balance is the most important single factor in athletic skiing and race technique. In Part 2 and in Chapter 25, we addressed numerous ways to improve balance—by assuring the proper alignment of our boots, and by training the muscles that support balance when skiing. With these needs well cared for, we are ready to consider specific balance issues on skis. Let's begin with a simple observation:

> When a racer is in balance, he is able to act.
> When a racer is out of balance, he must react.

The racer (or other skier) who is in balance chooses what he will do next. The racer who is out of balance must delay that movement and react first to balance problems. In ski racing, there is no time for delay. Specific numbers help us to understand:

It takes 3/10 of a second to raise and lower your hands from waist to shoulder height and back. How far do racers go in 3/10 of a second?

> At DH speed (60 mph)— 26 feet
> At GS speed (40 mph) — 17 feet
> At SL speed (20 mph) —   9 feet

Stop now, and think carefully about these numbers. At GS speed, if you are out of balance for the time it takes to raise and lower your arm, you travel 17 feet. When striving to maintain a line within *inches* of accuracy, 17 feet is a long way. All compromises of balance affect the precise application of edge and pressure that accurately control the path of your skis. Whenever you're out of balance, you sacrifice some degree of control.

Small errors compound quickly. If you miss your optimum line by 2 inches or 12, you may:

1. Be into chatter marks or ruts that destroy your rhythm and affect your line.
2. Be forced into tighter turns than desired. These may require skidding rather than carving.

Every deviation from a preferred line is exaggerated as you proceed down course. One small error leaves a racer subject to increasing difficulties. Balance problems often expand exponentially.

As we come to understand this phenomena, we appreciate the need for absolute precision in modern racing. Diann Roffe Steinrotter says, *"under the most difficult circumstances, you must be exact."* We like Diann's choice of the word "exact," and her focus on this aspect of racing. In most parts of modern race courses, there is neither time nor space for scrambling or balance recovery. In evaluating a racer's technique, it is useful to ask what percent of the time he or she is able to be exact. For the best racers, who are well balanced on their skis, the percentage is high. For those who are out of balance, the percentage is low. Diann says that if a World Cup racer is out of balance (or inexact) just once in a race, it is difficult to win.

It's instructive to stand within a few feet of the race line on a practice course at a World Cup event. The speed and precision of the athletes is much greater than one can appreciate by watching television or even standing fifty feet away behind a course barrier. From one turn to the next, there's no time for error, and no space for inexactness. To run a desired line, precise ski/snow contact must be maintained. The weight transfer from one turn to the next is incredibly fast. Precision is possible only with perfect balance.

What technical goals can we establish that contribute to good balance when racing? Let's look first at balance on the lateral plane, then at fore/aft balance.

LATERAL BALANCE

The most significant aid to lateral balance is the stability of a carving ski. Balance is tentative on a skidding ski, and relatively secure on a carving ski. It is most important to begin turns with a carving action. The smallest skid at turn initiation creates deceleration, a lack of stability, and a loss of exactness. These are serious penalties. If you begin with a skid, it is hard to stop skidding. If you begin with a carving action, it is much easier to continue the carving throughout the turn. Remember to *edge first,* then pressure.

Perfect canting contributes to balance in two ways. It provides the most functional and efficient stance, and it helps racers begin turns with a carving action.

A wider stance contributes to lateral balance. Many racers are skiing, *at times*, in a wider stance than is commonly seen among recreational skiers. They are also, *at times*, distributing their weight more evenly on both skis. This is most evident on flatter terrain and with long radius turns. The more even weight distribution aids gliding on softer snow. Please note how careful we have been to say "at times." Ski racing is an athletic event with infinite variables. The best athletes are creative and adaptable. They draw on a broad range of skills for different situations. One makes a serious mistake to say that a given technique or position on skis is always superior. We can identify trends that appear more common than a few years ago; but it would be misleading to suggest that any racer try to adapt a new skill to situations where it's not warranted.

A good example is the attention that has been given to skiing on two feet and using the inside ski in the past few years. Because a few World Cup skiers used these movements in selected turns, many racers thought there was a "new technique" and tried to apply two ski skills in situations that were not productive. These racers, and some of their coaches, were misled by exaggerated reports in the press about using the inside ski in new and dramatic ways.

The facts are: (1) the best racers still ski primarily on their outside or downhill ski; and (2) racers have been using their inside ski for all the years we've been watching, and for many years before that. Sometimes they do so when the terrain is easy and weighting both skis assists gliding, or a diverging step provides the smoothest transition between turns. In some difficult turns, racers use any edge they can get a grip with. It's easy enough to find pictures of racers with substantial weight on their inside ski, but . . .

When good racers are in good control, the more difficult the turn and terrain, the more likely they are to stand strongly on their downhill ski. The downhill ski is more stable and more balanced in almost all situations. It provides the best platform for angulation and strong edging.

Man is a two-legged animal. Good skiers can certainly ski on one foot or two, inside ski or outside; but "home base" is still on the downhill ski in 1993. Our analysis of physics and body mechanics suggests it will stay there for a long time to come.

FORE/AFT BALANCE

The critical issue in fore/aft balance is the position of the center of mass. As the CM is roughly in the hip area, we "see" or evaluate fore/aft balance as a position of the hips. A balanced stance should not be seen as a single position. In skiing, we are working with *dynamic balance*. This is defined as maintaining equilibrium *within a range of motion* with the fewest possible adjusting movements and muscle contractions.

Fore/aft balance is greatly influenced by boot function. If the boots place a skier in the back seat, the skier faces a constant struggle to stay centered in his range of motion. We assume, for now, that the boots are correctly aligned, and we are free to focus on technical choices. What position should a racer *choose* to ski in?

We can make some useful generalizations, but it's important these not be seen as absolutes for all racers in all turns. Course conditions, steepness of terrain, space between gates, etc. all affect the choices a racer makes. With this disclaimer, we can stress that a racer's "home position" should be neutral over his skis. We observe many racers who try too often to ski on the back of their skis. They think they can utilize the tail of the ski to increase their speed. At times, on flat terrain and easy turns, this may be helpful. For the great majority of turns, however, the best racers work from neutral to forward.

A study of the photos throughout this book shows a hip position that is forward at the top of the turn, and well centered in the belly of the turn. The best World Cup racers we have spoken with insist there is no time to recover from positions where the CM is aft of center. Diann Roffe Steinrotter says: "If you get behind center, you have to play catch-up; and there is no time for catch-up. To be exact, you must ski neutral and forward." Ove Nygren says simply: "*Every* turn begins on the balls of my feet."

The CM is the driving force in ski racing. At the top of the turn, you must have "sharp knees," and the hips driving to the inside and into the fall line. Photos 73 A and B (next page) show Marc Giardelli at the top of a slalom turn. These photos show the classic stance of a balanced modern racer. The knees and hips are clearly forward, and the torso is erect.

In the middle of racing turns, the CM is normally in a neutral position. This provides the optimum balance required for lateral weight transfer, divergent steps, or whatever movement is used to transition from one turn to the next.

At the end of easy turns where gates are widely spaced, racers often pressure the tail of the ski in subtle ways; but they do so without moving their CM into the back seat. Remember that the heel unit of a ski binding is well aft of the mid-point of a ski's running surface. You can transmit pressure through the heel of your boot (and to the tail of your ski) without moving your hips way back. Likewise, the AFD under the ball of the foot, is close to the mid-point of the running surface. This allows a skier to use forward leverage without getting too much on the forebody of the ski. Modern race skis are designed to perform efficiently when the athlete driving them is working his/her CM from neutral to forward. This arrangement best supports athletic movement and consistent balance.

A study of the best slalom skiers shows they often pressure the tail of the downhill ski when they step from it in a lateral or divergent step. This is a subtle move that creates some acceleration from muscle power and the rebound energy of the ski. Pressure can be applied to the tail of the ski from a surprisingly neutral position. (See photos 74 A and B.)

A final comment on fore/aft balance must be addressed to hand and arm positions. We observe a great many American racers reaching dramatically forward with their hands— often straightening their elbows. This movement is usually accompanied by a rounding or hunching forward of the shoulders. We see this position in Slalom, GS and Super G. The racers intent is to "drive forward" in a turn. If balance and agility are their goals, this is a questionable movement in most circumstances.

73A

73B

PHOTOS BY THOR KALLERUD

Marc Girardelli (LUX) has more than forty World Cup victories. He has been the most consistent skier on the men's tour for the past decade. In photo B he shows "sharp knees" and the hips well forward at the top of the turn. We have studied hundreds of photos of Marc, and have yet to see one where he is out of balance. He seems always relaxed and efficient. He shows a perfect combination of power with grace.

74A

74B

PHOTOS BY THOR KALLERUD

Photo A shows the end of a divergent step by Marc Giardelli. Note how the tail of his right ski is bent. Had the photo been taken a few hundredths of a second earlier, we would see more pressure on the tail of the ski and could better appreciate the "kick" he gets from this movement. In photo B, Marc is well balanced over the new outside ski, and ready to project his CM forward into the turn. Giardelli shows dynamic balance within a range of motion.

When the hands and shoulders are thrust forward, the hips move instinctively back to provide balance. Look again at the many photos in this book. The best racers stand with their shoulders square, not hunched, and their elbows are bent. This position allows them to drive forward with their hips or center of mass. It is more efficient and more powerful to drive with the center of mass than with the hands, arms, and shoulders. Note the hand and arm positions of Marc Giardelli in photos 73, 74, and 52.

It is difficult to know whether the "arms thrust forward syndrome" is a cause or an effect. If the hips are back because of poor alignment in the boots, then many racers will carry their hands and shoulders forward to compensate and maintain balance. This action is largely involuntary—an example of the body finding the easiest way to stay balanced. If racers are well balanced and then *choose* to drive with their hands (because they think it's a desirable technical goal), the hips must move back to balance this movement. Either way, the back seat is inefficient. If the goal is to be balanced, agile, and quick, the center of mass should be centered over the skis, and the arms and shoulders should be carried in a position that leaves the muscles of the upper torso relaxed.

REACTIONARY BALANCE : ANTICIPATORY BALANCE

There are two kinds of balance skiers should be aware of: *Reactionary Balance* and *Anticipatory Balance*. Most of the discussion on the previous pages has focused on reducing the need for reactionary balance adjustments. This is the use of the hands and arms, etc., to "get back in balance" or to adjust for changes in balance.

Anticipatory balance is especially interesting in sports like skiing where there is extensive dynamic movement. As you become more confident of the turns you can make with carving skills, you can anticipate balance needs by angulating before the turns begin. This process is a part of the trust required to edge first, then pressure your skis. For the most dynamic turns, large anticipatory movements must be made. For the most skillful skiers, movements of anticipatory balance are as instinctive and natural as reactionary balance adjustments, but they are not the same. For anticipatory balance, the adjustment *precedes* the forces of a turn rather than reacting to them. Thus, anticipatory balance is action. Reactionary balance is reaction. Action is better.

All movements that anticipate edging and angulation needs are examples of anticipatory balance on a lateral plane. Anticipatory balance is important on the fore/aft plane as well. Changes in pitch, ruts, bumps, etc., all require thinking ahead and balancing ahead. Downhillers approaching rolls, jumps, or major changes in pitch have a great need for anticipatory balance skills.

The USST Alpine Training Manual puts a strong emphasis on improving balance through skiing varied and challenging terrain. Experience is the best teacher. We applaud this emphasis, and encourage young skiers to train both in gates and in free skiing where balance demands are challenging.

BALANCE AND NEURO-MUSCULAR EFFICIENCY

When a muscle is busy doing one task, it is less efficient at doing others. This simple idea must be understood by all athletes who strive for efficiency and economy of motion. The principle is best illustrated with a simple exercise:

Place a book or magazine on the floor as an object to jump over. Your task is to jump laterally back and forth over this object as fast as possible. Stand beside the book and bend forward at the waist anywhere from 60 to 90 degrees. Then jump left and right across the book as quickly as you can. Next, stand with your torso erect, and jump ten times as fast as you can. Then bend at the waist and try again. Please, put this book down, and do this exercise now.

What do you learn? Your lateral movement is quicker when standing erect. Why?

When erect, your skeleton supports your upper body weight and allows your back muscles to relax. They have little work to do. When you begin to jump, the lower back muscles are free to assist your jumping task with no other responsibilities.

When you bend at the waist, your back muscles are engaged in the task of supporting your head, shoulders, chest, etc. As this task is ongoing when you begin to jump, the muscles are *not* entirely free to assist your jumping task. They *can* be employed, and they *will* work, but not as efficiently as before. They have two tasks now. Their efficiency at supporting the jumping task is diminished. The net result is that you jump more awkwardly and more slowly. The scientific explanation of this common sense idea is made clear in the text and drawings on pages 61 and 62.

In how many ways can we apply this principle to the tasks that confront a ski racer? Whenever balance is compromised and muscles must solve the problem, then relaxation, coordination, and speed of movement are reduced for all affected muscles. Look at pictures of Marc Girardelli and Karen Percy for excellent examples of a relaxed and well-balanced stance.

If your natural stance (controlled by your boot/suspension system) is less than perfect, then ***some*** muscles are ***always*** busy trying to achieve a balanced position. They are less than 100 percent efficient at performing other tasks. When any aspect of your technique requires continuous balance adjustment, you pay a price in efficiency. Consider undisciplined hand movements, a bent over stance, excessive rotary motion in turns, etc. The best skiers are those who accomplish the most with the least effort.

ECONOMY OF MOTION

The link between economy of motion and good balance is always close. As you strengthen one, you enhance the other. As balance improves, less movement is required for balance adjustment. This leaves more muscles available to work with maximum efficiency.

Efficiency is a primary goal of race technique. You must seek the largest response for the smallest effort. If you need a few degrees of edge, roll your ankle. If more edge is needed, knee angulation is quicker than hip angulation—but it's not as strong. When G forces are high, hip angulation or full-body inclination is needed. Quiet upper-body movement allows the best control of the ski through lower-body movement. At all times, do as little work as possible to achieve a desired result. Work smarter not harder.

Movement takes time. If we consider again that moving an arm from hip to shoulder and back takes 3/10 second, we can understand how much time is lost when body movements are excessive. Racers have no time to spare. The best racers exhibit extraordinary discipline and efficiency in upper body movement. All racers must learn to be smooth and functional in their skiing. Fluid motion is best. Abrupt movements should be avoided.

THE MASTERY OF CARVING SKILLS

One of the most important technical goals of modern racing is "to ski from arc to arc." All good racers can do this on flat to medium slopes. The challenge is to carve turns on increasingly steeper terrain. A racer who can carve where others are skidding, gains time.

Carving is fast. Skidding is slow. For developing racers, the critical skill is to begin turns without skidding. ***The fundamentals stressed in Parts 3, 4, and 5 must be learned before any success in racing can be achieved.*** Most important are learning to edge the ski first, then turn; and to ski with extreme edge angles.

Racers must start as many turns as possible with a pure carving motion. There must be no push, no skid, no scrubbing of snow. Racers must focus on this goal in free skiing as well as in race training.

It is not possible, of course, to carve all turns. Many racing turns are too sharp to pure carve. Racers must then make choices for what part of the turn to skid, and for how to accomplish the direction change required with the least deceleration. When turns are partly skidded, ski design is still used to generate turning forces. The goal is to carve as much of the turn as possible, and to exit the turn with the greatest possible speed. Skid when you have to, then establish edge lock as early as possible.

In the Tomba sequence (page 120) the turn in frame 2 is too sharp to pure carve. Tomba skids a little, but only briefly. Three elements of this turn deserve our attention.

> First, Tomba begins this turn with a carving action. He is patient at the top of the turn (frame 1), edging his skis and establishing a carving response. He approaches the difficult part of the turn (frame 2) with everything primed for a dramatic response. The skis are on edge. He has good angulation. His stance and balance are perfect.

> Second, when it is time to crank the turn, Tomba is in position to make his skis do the most possible work. He doesn't just push on the tails and skid around the cor-

ner. He drives his CM inside and forward; and he gets the ski edge to grip as well as possible on the tightest line possible. He takes full advantage of ski design to create turning forces.

Third, Tomba ends the turn with a clean edge lock and excellent acceleration toward the next gate.

To achieve strong edge angles early in a turn, "cross-under" skills and lateral flexibility are most important. Racers must be comfortable steering their skis on paths widely divergent from their center of mass. (Review pages 120–125). This movement can only be executed with confidence that the ski displaced far outside your center of mass will support you when the edge is engaged and pressure builds. These skills are learned in small increments. They should be developed first in free skiing, then applied in gate training.

FREE SKIING

It is important to ski with precision and with clear technical goals when free skiing. Every turn you make reinforces muscle memory patterns in the brain and CNS. Sloppy practice in free skiing leads to sloppy races. Good practice leads to good races. Two habits must be developed.

First, ***whenever you start down a mountain, seek the fall line and carve your first turn.*** Many skiers start slowly and do some kind of rhythm check with a skid and edge set in their first turn. This is a terrible habit for racers. Your first turn should be an accelerating movement. Make it your habit and instinct to seek speed in every first turn you make.

Second, when free skiing, "***pick a slow line and go fast on it.***" There are two ways to control speed on snow skis. One is to use your skis as brakes—skidding them sideways whenever you wish to go slower. The other is to turn further out of the fall line in each traverse. This controls speed by selection of line. Racers should use the second method whenever possible. It should be instinctive to seek speed and let your skis glide. *Braking maneuvers should be isolated and shut out of muscle memory patterns.* Braking skills are, of course, necessary to ski safely under some conditions. When braking is needed, it should be consciously used. Instinctive skiing should be focused on carving skills.

Skiers who have "a racer's heart" abhor skidding. When their skis begin to skid, every instinct of their mind and muscle is to end the skid as quickly as possible by establishing edge lock on the skidding ski.

Your authors are both ex-racers. We find it painfully difficult to ski behind friends who ride a skidding ski through long, sustained turns. We react the same way to this as hearing fingernails scratched across a blackboard. Stop! It invades the senses. Skis are made to carve, not skid. To use them constantly in long skidded turns abuses them. They chatter and vibrate, and so do your bones. It's more fluid and more pleasant to carve.

Though carving is more efficient, it is often hard work to pick a slow line and go fast on it. This approach requires active, precise, dynamic skiing. It requires working a line with much larger changes of direction. Though this may be hard work, *it is exhilarating work*. One of the primary joys of skiing is creating wonderful responses from your skis. If this takes extra effort, so be it. We love to make the ski carve, to feel it hold a difficult line, and then release into a new turn. We like to be masters of our skis, not passengers sliding on them. Sometimes we work so hard in free skiing that we get a physical and emotional "pump." For athletes, this is a good feeling.

The bottom line for racers is that they must learn to create and sustain speed in courses. This skill can be strengthened in all free skiing, if you stay focused on the goal.

As racing often requires the use of extreme edge angles, these should be explored in free skiing. To learn new skills, you have to experiment outside your comfort zone. This requires setting increasingly hard tasks in free skiing as well as in gate training. Try over and over again to carve ever sharper turns, to put the ski more and more on edge and make it hold.

In quick, short turns, use extreme knee angulation. In longer turns, if you have enough speed and centrifugal force, explore the limits of hip angulation and full body inclination. Try in fast parallel skiing to do goofy things that require extreme anticipatory balance. How much can you edge your skis and not fall down? How sharp a turn can you carve on a given slope at different speeds? Be playful and imaginative. Have contests with ski partners to see who can edge their skis most radically, or achieve the greatest angulation without falling. Look at the most dramatic photos of racers throughout this book, and try to duplicate the edge angles and angulation they achieve.

Many racers fail to make constructive use of free skiing time. It is good, often, to just relax and play on the mountain. But it's also good to use free skiing to develop racing skills. To do so requires imagination, focusing on a task, and creating difficult challenges. Ove Nygren does "ten turn exercises" when free skiing. He sets a specific task or goal, makes ten turns as perfectly as he can, and stops. He then sets another task, and tries to make ten more perfect turns.

The above approaches that help racers are equally useful for recreational skiers. Racing is not a different way of skiing. A race course is simply a defined challenge, a fair test of the most advanced skiing skills. Athletic skiers, whether racers or all-mountain skiers, have the same needs to master carving skills.

THE DEVELOPMENT OF ATHLETIC MOVEMENT

As athletes, equipment, and training methods improve, alpine racing is becoming an increasingly athletic event. Quickness, agility, and power are required to become a champion. Success depends on four components:

1. Physical conditioning. This includes strength, flexibility, quickness, and agility. Racers with high goals must pay their dues in year-round training. Given equal technique and equipment, the racer with the greatest strength will consistently win. The recent success of the Norwegian team has not been based on a new technique or equipment advantage. The Norwegians have beaten their competitors in physical training. They have increased their strength training volume to higher levels than other national programs. Strength is their trump card. They have paid their dues and earned their victories.

2. Better "Cleats." Skis are improving every year. Sharper and quicker carved turns are possible. Shock absorbent binding systems have enhanced ski performance. Racers must learn to fully utilize the power and potential of new skis and boot/binding systems. Taken together, these tools are like extra-long cleats. They provide racers with stable platforms for athletic movement.

3. Better Balance. All concepts in this book that contribute to superior balance increase a skier's capacity for athletic movement. The better balanced skiers are, the more athletic they can be.

4. Efficient Technique / Power with Grace. Racing technique is evolving constantly from the best skiers in the world. The direction of progress is toward power with grace. Power alone can't win, nor can efficient technique without power. The future belongs to those who best combine the two. All progressive thinking about "new" or "better" ways to ski must focus on the union of strength, efficiency, and the laws of motion.

As with all sports, the rate of technical innovation is slowing down as we approach an understanding of optimum efficiency. This is most easily measured in sports like swimming where record performances can be measured on a consistent "playing field." Swim coaches are still learning about efficient technique and physical training, but they are getting so close to perfection that the rate of progress will continue to slow for the foreseeable future. Skiing has more room to grow because we can develop new equipment and related techniques to exploit it. Swim suits can't get much faster. Skis can. The apparent direction in ski design is to improve carving and edge hold possibilities. The technical adjustments that follow will demand full exploitation of the carving potential of the skis. These developments will increase the pleasures of skiing for all athletic skiers.

THE UTILIZATION OF GRAVITY

Gravity is the driving force in ski racing. It provides at least 95 percent of our power. At slower speeds, when we can step or skate, we are able to generate some speed from muscle recruitment and ski rebound, but these resources are of small significance in determining a racer's speed. Thoughtful coaches are focusing increasingly on ways to better utilize the forces of gravity.

The pull of gravity is constant and equal at all times for all skiers. Whether you make good use of gravity or dissipate it's force determines your speed. Braking, caused by skidding, is the primary decelerating force in skiing. Braking varies at all times for all racers. No racer can increase the power of gravity. Braking forces, however, are always subject to change through a racers action. As net speed is the sum of accelerating and decelerating forces, the key to going faster is staying off the brake. This is why it is so important to begin turns without skidding.

When thinking of ways to best use the forces of gravity, it is most helpful to think of gravity working on a skier's center of mass. For any given race course, there is a particular line that provides the greatest possible acceleration for the center of mass. The closer to the fall line the CM stays, the faster you go. As you turn the CM out of the fall line, you slow down. To best utilize gravity, the CM should follow the shortest possible path, and should remain as close to the fall line as possible. The shortest line, however, may require skidding of the skis and the braking this causes. ***Racers must find the best compromise between the optimum line for their CM (as regards gravity), and the optimum line for their skis to avoid skidding***. Both masters are best served when there is a divergence of ski line and body line. Look again at photos 73, 74, and 52. In each of these turns, Girardelli's skis take the rounder path which allows for the best carving and the least deceleration. At the same time his body follows the direct line where gravity provides the most acceleration. Look also at the photo sequence of Tomba on page 122.

The greatest efficiency occurs here when the CM is ahead of the skis at the top of the turn. You can't be playing catch-up with your center of mass. You must lead with it. It makes no more sense to try and ski athletically with your CM trailing your feet than to try and run dry land slalom courses that way in soccer shoes. The CM must be neutral or forward at the start of each turn so you can project that mass on the most efficient line.

A final idea that thoughtful World Cup racers have expressed to us broadens our understanding of gravity. "The mountain creates speed. The racer harnesses it." This concept reflects a fundamental change in racing over the past decade. We used to think that a racer had to "create" speed. Step turns that utilized muscle power were important. Trying to flex the tail of the ski to create acceleration was a focus of many racers. Today's courses are set in a way that the challenge is less to create speed than to manage it. Gravity provides all the speed necessary. *The racers task is not to waste the gift*. Skidding dissipates speed, and wastes the gift. A poor choice of line gives away speed as well. Racers in the start gate should have an awareness that they are given a precise and limited amount of power (gravity) which they can use efficiently or waste.

One of the wisest coaches we have talked with says that in developing a strategy for racing, ***"it is more important not to lose time than to gain time."*** This concept deserves careful consideration. It applies especially to issues of balance, economy of motion, carving skills, and the utilization of gravity. It is a direct way of asserting that racers have only a small ability to control accelerating forces, but they have a great deal of control over decelerating forces. The problem is not so much how to speed up in ski racing, but how to avoid slowing down. In this regard, ski racing is like racing coaster-carts. Gravity provides the same power to all competitors. The cart with the least resistance goes the fastest.

There are only small opportunities in any course to really gain time, or to create acceleration. There are many, many opportunities to lose time. Every diversion from an optimum line is a loss of time. Every extraneous upper-body movement causes a loss of "exactness." Every skidding of the skis causes a dissipation of speed. Thus, the key to going faster is staying off the brake, and efficiently managing the accelerating force which gravity provides. The fastest skier is the one who combines the best line with the least braking.

Chapter 37

CARVING AT THE TOP OF THE TURN

A primary goal for all racers is to ski from arc to arc—to maximize the use of carving skills and to minimize skidding. Success in this endeavor depends on technique and choice of line. The technical skills required to begin turns without skidding have been addressed in earlier parts of this book. Racers must learn to edge first, then use pressure and steering to create carved turns. RR Turn exercises are great aids to learning how to carve at the top of the turn. All of these skills are made easier with proper balance and suspension system alignment.

Once these skills are learned, the choice of line becomes a critical factor in carving the early part of a turn. If you lack patience at the start of a turn, and try to turn too sharp, you will skid. If you select a line that requires too tight an arc at turn initiation, you'll skid again. If you turn too early before a gate and leave too much of the turn to be finished under the gate, you'll skid once more and decelerate rapidly.

To construct a concept of the most efficient line for racing, we must answer two questions:

1. What turn shape best facilitates carving?
2. What line on a race course best facilitates carving?

Let's look first at turn shape.

THE COMMA TURN

Gravity and the *Inclination of the Slope* affect all turns. They offer help in the entry (pre fall-line) phase of most turns, and they create problems in the exit (post fall-line) phase. *The steeper the hill the more this holds true.* On steep terrain, gravity has a large influence on turn shape. On flatter terrain, this influence becomes less significant. A study of drawing 19 makes these concepts clear.

In the entry phase, gravity pulls your body to the inside of the turn. This partially neutralizes centrifugal force, and reduces your tendency to skid.

In the fall-line phase, gravity has little effect on centrifugal force or skidding. Gravity does, however, increase your speed through the fall-line. This added speed increases centrifugal force in the next phase of the turn.

In the exit phase, both gravity and centrifugal force pull skiers to the outside of their turning arc. This increases the forces that cause skidding.

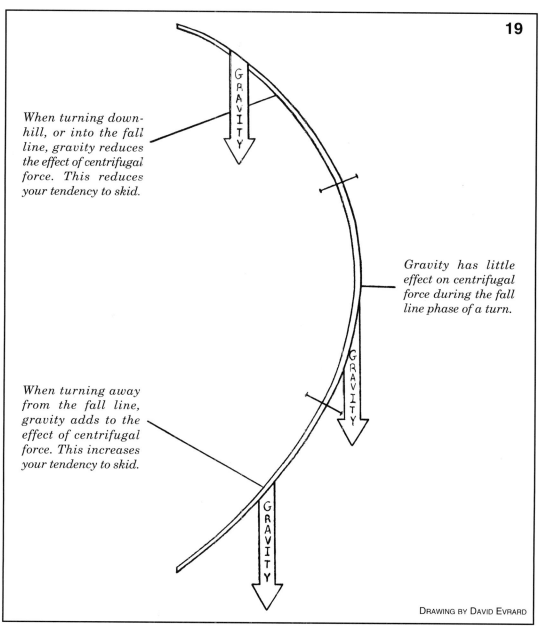

19

When turning down-hill, or into the fall line, gravity reduces the effect of centrifugal force. This reduces your tendency to skid.

Gravity has little effect on centrifugal force during the fall line phase of a turn.

When turning away from the fall line, gravity adds to the effect of centrifugal force. This increases your tendency to skid.

DRAWING BY DAVID EVRARD

HOW GRAVITY AFFECTS A SKI TURN

Gravity is a constant force, but its accelerating power increases as a slope grows steeper. Centrifugal force changes with speed and turning radius. These forces are different in all turns. Still it is useful to consider a hypothetical turn. Let's assume for a given turn that centrifugal force exerts 4 units of pull and gravity exerts 2 units. In the entry phase, the net forces pulling you to the outside of the turn are 4 (CF) minus 2 (G) equals 2. In the exit phase, the sum of the forces is 4 (CF) plus 2(G) equals 6. Your tendency to skid is thus three times greater in the exit phase of the turn than in the entry phase. These numbers are only hypothetical and are for two points in a single turn. The concept, however, should be clear: ***it's easier to carve without skidding in the entry phase of a turn than in the exit phase.***

Gravity isn't your only friend in the entry phase. For most turns, *the slope of the mountain works for you too.* In the entry phase, it's tilted toward the inside of the turn like a banked turn at an auto racing oval, or a bicycling velodrome. In the exit phase, the slope works against you. After passing through the fall-line, you must cope with a "fall-away" slope. Carving on the fall away is far more difficult than when the hill is banked in your favor.

Good skiers, because they are skillful at skiing on steep hills, *underestimate* the relative difficulty of turning in the exit phase of a turn. To better appreciate the role of the slope in a turn, imagine running the same course in summer months on a mountain bike. How much easier is it to turn the bike downhill (in the entry phase) than to control the turn after passing through the fall-line? The difficulties seem more clear when we think of the bike, but the forces are equal in skiing. The laws of physics are the same in January and July.

The concepts represented in drawing 19 apply to all turns and should be understood by all racers. Remember that the steeper the slope, the greater the influence of gravity. Consider these implications:

A. It's easier to turn without skidding in the entry phase than the exit phase.

B. The sharpest part of turns should be made in the entry and fall-line phase, not in the exit phase.

C. Speed gained in the fall-line phase is best sustained if you don't turn too sharp in the exit phase.

D. Lengthening the radius of a turn as you progress into the exit phase helps to accomplish C.

E. Any way you can lengthen the fall-line phase increases the time period when gravity provides the most acceleration.

Putting all of these concepts together, it is clear that the most efficient turn is shaped like a comma—a tight radius at the top, and a straighter tail at the bottom. When choosing the most efficient line in a race course, the advantages of a comma turn should be heavily weighed.

If a sharp, carved turn is to be made at the top of the comma, it is evident that racers must be skilled at first edging and then pressuring their skis. The ability to achieve substantial edge angles early in a turn—without skidding—is critical for racing success.

All of these concepts apply to recreational skiing. The easiest way to ski is to turn hard before the fall-line, and to lengthen your turn radius after passing through the fall-line. In this way, you can consistently use gravity and the slope to your advantage.

THE "RISE-LINE" SECRET

One of the fascinations of ski racing is that every turn offers a new challenge. Speed, terrain, arc, and snow conditions are constantly changing. Racers must choose a precise line for every turn. These choices are made with lightening speed while progressing down a course. Every turn is different. Each individual racer has unique skills to apply to his or her task. The best line for one racer may be impossible for another.

For every turn, each individual athlete must choose the optimum line for his or her ability. As writers or coaches, far removed from this action, we cannot possibly define "the best line" for any specific turn. We can, however, present a concept that applies to a majority of racing turns. Racers who understand this concept, and make line choices based on it, have a significant advantage.

When Diann Roffe won the World Championship Giant Slalom in 1985, she was an 18-year-old senior at Burke Mountain Academy. When we study films of that race, it is clear that Diann skied a more efficient line than the World Cup veterans whom she beat. It was a line she learned from her Burke coaches. When Diann won the Silver Medal in Giant Slalom at the '92 Olympics, she was still adhering to that classic line. Approaching the '94 Olympics, she says: "Despite all the changes in skis, technique, and course-setting, the rise-line concept still works."

What is this concept? And how does it relate to drawing 21 and the comma turn?

Simply stated: ***For most racing turns, the major direction change should begin at the moment you cross the fall line extended above the gate you're approaching.*** To simplify our language, we call the fall-line extended above the gate the "rise-line." (See drawing 20, next page.)

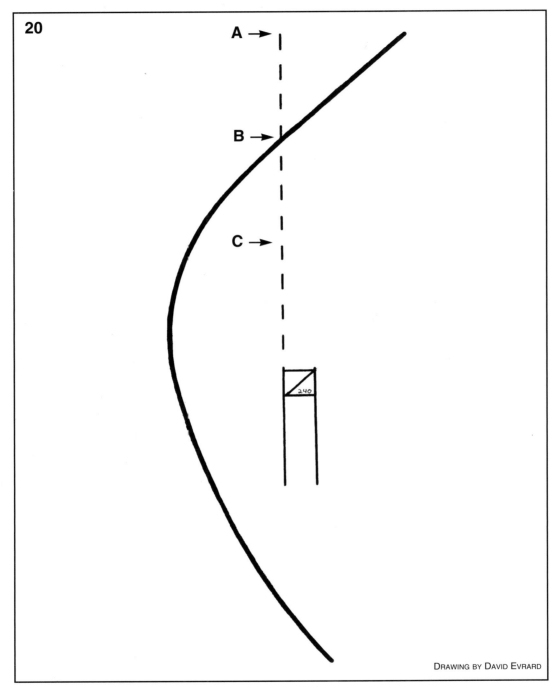

RISE-LINE

The dotted line is the rise-line.
The solid line is the path of the racer's outside ski.

Drawing by David Evrard

The challenge for racers is to discipline themselves to wait for the rise-line before starting the major direction change of their skis. For almost all skiers, this is *not* a natural instinct. ***Waiting for the rise-line must be learned through conscious and disciplined effort.*** The natural instinct is to turn your skis toward the gate before reaching the rise-line.

When faced with the speed and difficulty common to race courses, a racer's instinct is to get a head start on each turn. "Anticipate." "Turn early." "Be prepared." "Don't wait until the last possible second." These are all natural impulses; but if they cause you to turn your skis too early, they are counter productive.

Photos 75A,B,C and 76A,B,C (next pages) show two racers at a critical gate in the 1992 Olympic Super G. Paul Accola (SUI) carves a clean arc past the gate because he waited for the rise-line. Urs Kalin (SUI) starts his turn far inside of Accola's line (which is clearly visible in the snow), and must then skid sideways to clear the pole.

To understand the difference in these two approaches to the gate, focus your attention on each skier's right ski. In 75A, Accola's right ski is tracking on an arc that he will follow in a consistent carve throughout the turn. Kalin, cheating on the rise line, turns his right ski too early. In 76A, his right ski is pointed straight at the gate. If he continues to carve a turn from this position, he will turn inside the gate. In 76B, Kalin has begun to skid sideways. In 76C, he has actually turned his ski 15 degrees to the right in order not to pass too close to the gate.

Waiting for the rise-line is delaying the turn of your skis until the last possible moment. The result is that you can carve aggressively, make a good comma turn, and carry your speed on a carving ski below the gate. Racers who cheat on the rise line make a "J turn"— straight at the top and sharp at the bottom. Because they start the turn too early, they have to skid laterally to avoid turning inside the pole. They are left having to complete a sharper turn under the gate where gravity and the slope of the hill work against them. When you cheat on the rise-line, you lose speed at both ends of the turn. Racers who wait for the rise-line eliminate the problems evident in the photos of Kalin.

75A

Paul Accola
waits for the
rise line,

75B

carves
cleanly past
the pole,

75C

and exits the
turn on a
carving ski.

PHOTOS BY THOR KALLERUD

76A

Urs Kalin
turns his skis
too early,

76B

skids
sideways to
clear the
pole,

76C

and will have
difficulty
carving
beneath the
gate.

PHOTOS BY THOR KALLERUD

75D

76D

The completion phase of a turn reveals the success or failure of the chosen line.
Photos 75D and 76D show Accola and Kalin three frames (.6 seconds) later. Accola has finished his turn and is stepping to his left ski. Kalin is still skidding on his right ski. Look
at the bush which is almost hidden behind Accola, but is far in front of Kalin. This land-
mark shows how much Accola has gained in a 1.2-second section of this course. In the
last frame, it is clear that Accola has a better line and more speed. His net gain will
increase at least through the next turn. Kalin's mistake was turning his skis toward the
gate before reaching the rise-line.

Skiers who wait for the rise-line, like Hans Pieren (SUI) in photo 77 (next pages), eliminate skidding before the gate, or having to turn too sharp below it. They maintain their
speed on a carving ski.

Waiting for the rise-line is an incredibly simple concept, but few racers understand it
well or execute it consistently. Surprisingly, it is taught by very few coaches. Look again
at photo 77A, and in your imagination turn Pieren's skis so they point straight at the
inside pole. Had he cheated on the rise-line, this is the position he would be in. Can you
now imagine the path his skis would have to follow through the rest of the turn? It should
be clear how large an influence rise line timing has on speed.

It is instructive to study race films and rank the first seed competitors on how well
they wait for the rise-line, then compare this ranking with the race finish order. The rise-
line ranking and the finish order are remarkably similar. The racer wins whose rise-line
timing is best. The next best adherent to the rise-line principle finishes second, etc. This
sounds terribly simplistic in a sport with so many variables as ski racing. We insist, however, the correlation is very close. Large technical errors, and repeating small ones, are
invariably preceded by failures to wait for the rise-line. This principle holds true at *all*
levels of racing—from Buddy Werner League to the World Cup.

Two skills must be integrated with waiting for the rise-line. First, you must understand that you do not *begin* your turn when you get to the rise-line. You prepare early
with edge change, weight shift, anticipatory balance, etc. You get the ski on edge and
glide on it. You get your body in position to turn aggressively, but you wait. (Photo 77A)
Then, when you reach the rise line, you pressure the ski and turn aggressively. In short,
you must be well prepared and "waiting to pounce." When you get to the rise-line, step on
it and go (photo 77B).

Second, please note that the rise-line is not a single spot. It is a long line that can be
intercepted higher or lower above the gate. Look again at drawing 20 and imagine a high-
line (intersect at A), middle-line (intersect at B), and low-line (intersect at C). A comma
turn can start on the rise-line at each of these points. Which intersect point would be
fastest?

There is, of course, no right answer. In general, stronger and more skillful skiers can
intersect the rise-line at a lower point and not get jammed below the gate. The lower intersect allows for a straighter line between gates and more time close to the fall-line. This

These four photos perfectly demonstrate waiting for the rise-line. Look at Pieren's right ski in photo A. He is very patient in turning this ski. It is well on edge, and he is ready to begin a clean carving action as he crosses the rise-line. From A to B, the top of the comma, Pieren carves on a very clean edge. He lets the ski run in the fall line (C), and is able to carve through the exit phase of the turn (D).

77C

77D

provides more speed, but you must have the strength and skill to carve the ensuing turn in the shorter space that remains.

Each individual racer must choose how far above each gate to intersect the rise-line. ***Speed, terrain, snow conditions, location of the following gates, and the skier's ability influence how high the intersect should be made.*** Amidst many changing variables, one principle is constant: If you "cheat" on the rise-line, turning your skis too early toward the gate, you will skid before and after the gate, and go slower. If you wait for the rise-line, you can carve cleaner turns and maintain your speed. Remember the adage that it is more important not to lose speed than to gain speed. Cheating on the rise-line is a quick way to lose speed.

The rise-line principle applies most easily to Giant Slalom, but it works for most turns in Slalom and Super G as well. Downhill turns are so long that it's sometimes hard to picture the rise-line so far above a gate. Still, the principle holds for *many, many* DH turns.

We quoted Diann Roffe Steinrotter as saying, "The rise-line principle still works." She went further in our interview to say that with today's skis (that turn so sharply) she often goes *beyond* the rise-line. She also goes higher up the line than she did a few years ago— in an effort to stay ahead of the course, and to get more work done above the gate. What is "high" for a racer of Diann's ability, however, may be dangerously low for most developing racers.

Breakaway poles significantly alter the choice of line racers can make at each gate. In most slalom turns (and many GS), it is obviously best to run your skis as close to the pole as possible and to simply "run through" or deflect the pole with your body. For other GS and most Super G turns, avoiding the pole is still the wise choice. The line of the skis must be far enough from the pole to allow the body room to angulate. The important skill then becomes to approach the pole on a line (***think ski tracks***) that allows the skis to carve a pure arc before and while passing the pole. Don't aim too close to the pole and have to skid your feet out at the last moment. Such a skid always scrubs away speed.

In the era before breakaway poles, the skill of leaving room for angulation had to be exercised in almost all turns. Even so, it was a difficult skill to teach. The problem is more difficult now because for so many gates it's best to run your skis as close to the pole as possible. Today's racers must constantly shift from skiing *through* poles to skiing *around* them. At racing speeds, these adjustments are difficult. This offers one more opportunity for the intelligent skier to gain an advantage. The key is to understand that the line of the skis and the line of the center of mass are distinctly different.

Accomplished racers "see" both of these lines as clearly distinct. They are always aware of the line their CM is taking, and the line their skis are following. A review of the photos of racers throughout this book shows a clear difference between these lines. Look carefully at these photos and imagine yourself in the racers' position. Can you sense the two lines? Learning to do so is a critical skill for all ski racers.

In closing, we need to emphasize again the diversity that applies to all issues of line selection. Speed, snow conditions, following gates, and racer skills determine the best line for each racer at each gate. The best line for one racer may not be efficient for another. The same racer, on two successive runs, may make different line choices based on speed, balance, and snow conditions that are always changing. As racers gain strength and improve their skills, they can carve on tighter arcs and at higher speeds. The many variables in ski racing keep it interesting and challenging for all competitors.

JULIE LEWIS

"On-hill baggage includes radio, poles, drills, wrenches, video cameras, timing gear, and clothing bags."

PART 10

PERSPECTIVES FOR COACHES

A good case can be made that alpine skiing is the most difficult of all sports to coach. The environment is cold, and sometimes hostile. Travel logistics (with equipment) are imposing. On-hill baggage includes radio, poles, drills, wrenches, video cameras, timing gear, and clothing bags.

Coaches responsibilities run the gamut from off-snow training to on-snow coaching, course setting, equipment modification, tracking FIS points and qualifying procedures, attending seeding meetings, and managing contacts between racers and suppliers. In their spare time, they conduct races and fund raisers, deal with parents, and attend ski association committee meetings. How can one person do all these things, and do them well?

In contrast, a swimming coach can travel around the world with a stop watch in one pocket and a nylon bikini in the other. The water at all training sites is level, and every turn is 180 degrees. So why do people coach skiing? Because the play time (if you can find any) is more fun and the task is more challenging.

We offer these perspectives to honor all alpine coaches, and to make clear our understanding of the challenges they face. As we offer suggestions in the next four chapters, we want coaches to know that we understand the difficulties of their task. We write with humility and respect, but also with a faith that ski coaching, as a profession, is barely at a middle stage of development. We have a lot to learn.

Chapter 38

WHAT DO WE KNOW?

Most ski coaches, whether working for national teams or development programs, have been coaching "by the seat of their pants" for a long time. The truth is we don't *know* very much. Jarle Aamboe, Director of the Norwegian National Program, says, "Knowledge is a very important success factor. Granted *theoretical knowledge and research are dreadfully limited in alpine skiing*, we have tried to utilize and take advantage of the resources that are available." (Our italics.)

To gain some perspective, we urge ski coaches to read *Swimming into the 21st Century,* by Cecil M. Colwin. This thoughtful and comprehensive book leaves a distinct impression that swimming coaches know a lot more about swimming than ski coaches know about skiing. We should be challenged to catch up.

Swimming coaches have some advantages. They work in a controlled environment. Their athletes can be tested day after day on a consistent course. Some coaches have tenured university positions with associated research facilities. Most of the research that has been done world-wide has been shared between nations. As we see the scope of research and the conditions that support it, we might plan programs for skiing that would produce equally useful knowledge.

Swimming has profited greatly from the work of university coaches like Robert Kiphuth at Yale and "Doc" Counsilman at Indiana. These men, and others like them, have been excellent "intuitive coaches," and at the same time disciplined research scientists. Many have advanced degrees in physiology, sports training, or related fields. They have also been smart enough to get other scientists and researchers to help them. We need such leaders in American and world ski coaching.

For both long and short-term studies, the USST and USSCA have scarcely tapped the research capabilities of American Universities with strong ski programs, or of the ski academies which have access to controlled groups of racers. Because of their geographical affinity, the Ski Team has begun to use the University of Utah as a significant resource. This is one small step in the right direction, but many more steps need to be taken.

The primary focus of knowledge gathering for ski training has been related to off-snow conditioning. Here we have piggy-backed on the work done by running, biking, and strength coaches. By contrast, very little has been done to study on-snow issues.

Present computer technology offers many opportunities to do specific research on efficiency of line, use of gravity, balance and movement patterns, and foot function in various types of boots. Compared to swimming, or to track and field, there are enormous difficulties in measuring performance efficiency in snow skiing. The variables of terrain and equipment make "accurate analysis" difficult. These challenges, however, should not deter us from stronger efforts to learn some things we ought to know.

What would we like to know? We'd start with better understandings of feet and boots. What performance gains do orthotics provide? How much loose adaptation in the boot best meets the needs of racing? What affects does canting have for racers with different strength levels, for different snow conditions, and for different events? How much are reaction times slowed by skiing bent at the waist? At what speed does decreasing wind resistance become more important than improving agility? What gains or losses result from working the tail of the ski? What are the relative efficiencies of the comma turn on slopes of varying pitch? Intuitive coaches and athletes make good guesses on some of these questions. Other questions we have no answers for.

The ignorance of American coaches on canting issues, alignment, and balance is nearly universal, but there is even less knowledge among coaches from most of the European nations. (See footnote on page 237.) Are there opportunities for American coaches to lead the world in significant areas of stance and balance research? We think so. Over the past year, we have done as much thinking about suspension system issues as any coaches in the world. Our efforts have increased our understanding of how little we know, and of how little data is available to help us learn. Intuitive experience is a good teacher here, but hard science is needed as well.

American coaches should appreciate the opportunities open to them for significant research. There are many areas where it's possible to progress beyond "seat of the pants" or intuitive coaching. If we begin to understand how little we know about some critical issues in ski racing, we should then be motivated to expand our knowledge base. Does anyone have the time, the interest, and the necessary skills to help us learn?

Chapter 39

BEFORE "COACHING"

When a ski coach looks in a mirror, what does he see? An administrator? A course setter? A "hill coach" with a gift for teaching carving skills? A travel agent? A keen student of bio-mechanics and physics? An expert boot-fitter? A good shop mechanic? How many skills does a good coach need?

It's clear that no coach can excel on all fronts. If we leave administrative roles out of the picture, what are the most important coach to athlete skills? What services can coaches provide that contribute most to their athletes' performance?

Remember the wisdom of Charly Kahr: "The boots give you two seconds." We have focused on suspension issues throughout this book, so it isn't necessary to review the methods or purpose of providing skiers with optimum balance. A special perspective is, however, appropriate for coaches.

Just as racers want to compete head to head on snow, not in the boot-lab, we understand that coaches want to coach on snow. By training, habit, and instinct, coaches want to tell athletes how to stand, how to move, how to hold their hands, how to angulate, how to "go faster." In short, coaches want to teach ski racing skills—technique first, then line and tactics. We encourage coaches to swallow their pride, overcome their instincts, and "coach" first in the boot lab.

Providing perfect alignment and balance to a racer is the most important aspect of coaching. If this is not done first, then whatever "technical coaching" is done on the hill is teaching athletes to compensate. If *perfect* balance is not provided first, an athlete's potential is seriously limited.

The hard fact is that 90 percent of all the racers in the world are limited by balance restrictions. Of the 10 percent who are well balanced, one-half were born with an ideal physiology for the equipment they are using; and the other half have been fortunate to have a wise coach. *Every* coach must accept responsibility for providing the best possible boots, balance, and suspension system to his or her athletes.

To do so requires knowledge, time, effort, and an organized program. Coaches must provide these or struggle continually with coaching racers who are out of balance. Those who are out of balance to the rear will almost always hunch over at the waist. A coach can tell such athletes to stand more erect twenty times a day for a hundred days—and the athletes can't do it. If proper alignment is provided first in the boot lab, the athletes will stand erect without ever being told. *This approach is good coaching.* Most importantly, when perfect balance is provided (on both the lateral and fore/aft planes), then coaches are free to concentrate on the important skills that help racers to go faster.

We don't want to labor over this idea in the final pages of this book, but we have watched 95 percent of the coaches in America duck this responsibility for twenty years. We hope this book provides the knowledge and motivation coaches need to get the job done, and done right. We don't care how many other things coaches have to do, or how many ways they can justify the importance of their tasks. If they haven't provided good balance to their athletes, they have failed in the most fundamental responsibility that coaches have. Athletic skiing demands perfect balance. Coaches must help their racers find it.

In the spirit of teamwork and racer responsibility set forth in Chapter 33, it's important that coaches do more than provide alignment services to their athletes. Coaches should help all racers to fully understand the alignment process, and to become self-sufficient in meeting their balance needs.

Coaches need to learn everything they can about feet, boots, bindings, and suspension systems, then share this knowledge with the athletes they are coaching. For coaches who do this right, there are many rewards: their athletes progress quickly, perform well, finish often, and can explore their full potential.*

---

*Footnote (June 1994): Although canting issues are not yet widely understood among Austrian coaches, the National Team Men's coaching staff did careful canting work with all their athletes in 1994. This included early season evaluations, frequent timed run experiments, and continuous checking throughout the season..

They have reported to us that all their technical skiers are canted one to two degrees inside as we recommend in this book. Is there a connection between Austria's winning the Nation's Cup by a substantial margin in '94 and the attention they have given to canting? We think there is. Proper canting provides not only fast and efficient skiing; it also reduces the incidence of falling. Speed plus high finish rates equals many Nation's Cup points. There are, of course, many factors other than attention to canting that contribute to the Austrians' success. We just think that proper canting is a significant element in their success; and we know that few if any other teams (the U.S. included) have paid as much attention to "the suspension system" as have the Austrians in 1994.

We appreciate that the Austrian Head Coaches and Alpine Program Director have been careful readers of this book.

Chapter 40

RACER EVALUATION

Throughout this book, we have shown a respect for individuality in the style of athletic skiers. No two bodies are built the same, or work the same. Each racer must have the freedom to explore many ways of skiing, and to discover those that best harness the laws of physics—for his or her body. Through selected photographs, we have demonstrated good balance, carving skills, agility, and other traits that are common to athletic skiers. We have never, however, said that one skier's style or stance was "the best" or should be exactly copied. We have used photos to show skills that must be learned, but each athlete must learn them in slightly different ways.

We've admonished ski schools and PSIA examiners for too narrowly defining "correct" ways to ski or to demonstrate specific turns. If we show respect for individuality, do we run a risk of lacking standards? Will anarchy and a loss of discipline result? Can racers know "how well they are doing" if no standards are applied? Can we develop a "report card" that helps coaches and racers to establish useful goals and know if they are reaching them?

Let's turn to Burke Mountain Academy for help. On the page opposite is Burke's racer evaluation form. This was developed by Tomas Karlsson who is now the Head Coach at Burke. He was previously Head Coach of the Swedish Women's Team, and served as Sweden's Alpine Program Director from 1987 to 1992.*

This form is focused on the basic skills of skiing. It provides coaches and racers a straightforward way to evaluate where they are, and where they are trying to go.

One could develop more extensive forms that measure everything from edge sharpening skills to being on time for the bus, but Burke coaches are happy to stay focused on these fundamentals. We think they'd work well for PSIA exams, and for teacher/student evaluations in many ski school settings. When you get the fundamentals right, athletic skiing is easier than it looks.

* In April of 1994, Tomas Karlsson was appointed Head Men's Coach for the U.S. Ski Team.

BURKE MOUNTAIN ACADEMY   RACER EVALUATION FORM

1. BALANCE

           back   CENTER   front

- Fore and aft: _____

- Side to side: _____

Arms? busy: _____ CALM: _____ close to body: _____ OUT FROM BODY: _____

Shoulders? PARALLEL WITH SNOW: _____ tipping in: _____

Stance? narrow: _____ NATURAL: _____ wide: _____

Comments:_____

2. BODY DIRECTION / EDGING

      rotation   CALM   counter rotation

- Upper body: _____

      not enough   FINE   too much

- Edging with   Ankles _____

                Knees _____

                Hip _____

Comments:_____

3. WEIGHT DISTRIBUTION

      one ski   SWITCHING   two skis

- Between 1 or 2 skis _____

      no movements   FINE   too much

- Front to back _____

Comments:_____

4. CHANGING PRESSURE

      too static   FINE   too much

- Resisting and extending _____

      too early   FINE   to late

- Timing _____

Comments:_____

5. TACTICS / LINE

      too straight   FINE   too round

- Slalom _____

- Giant Slalom _____

Comments:_____

Chapter 41

THE COACH AS TEACHER AND LEARNER

In Chapter 32 we urged racers to be forever curious and always learning. Now we encourage coaches to approach skiing with the same goals.

Coaches play different roles at each level of skiing. Age group coaches working with racers from 10 to 14 have different responsibilities to their athletes than national team coaches. There are, however, important similarities. We have a tremendous respect for coaches who continue throughout their careers to learn and teach in two specific areas. First is keeping up to date with equipment developments; second is sharing a love for skiing with each of the athletes they coach.

The oldest of your authors has had an especially long career in both snow skiing and water skiing. As a water ski coach in his mid fifties, Warren continued to compete at the highest levels of the sport and to coach world-class competitors. To better understand the performance potentials they were working with, he devoted a great deal of time to skiing on the same models of skis his athletes were using. In slalom, he experimented constantly with different lines and techniques that weren't natural for his own skiing, but were best for those he coached. By "putting himself in the other persons body," he was best able to help his athletes get the most from their equipment, and from the techniques that were natural to them. As a bonus, he broadened his own experience, developed a variety of new skills, and continually nurtured his curiosity. When he retired from competitive water skiing at age 55, he was skiing at the highest performance level of his 38-year career.

Snow skiing offers similar opportunities for coaches to experiment with the equipment their racers are using. As a part of their research for this book, your authors spent four days at on-snow trade fairs in 1993. We skied on forty different pairs of skis and a variety of boots. The difference in ski performance was much greater than most people imagine. There's a common perception that "all skis are good now." There are, indeed, a great many *good* skis, but a few are *exceptional*. Good coaches should have a feel for the performance potential of the very best skis their athletes are using. It helps, also, to know how Rossignols differ from Salomons, Blizzards, or Elans, etc. Each ski has unique characteristics that may work better for one type of racer than another.

Doing equipment research may be most productive for those coaches who are exceptional skiers, but it is useful for *all* coaches. *There is always something to learn* when experimenting with equipment.

At the very least, coaches should ski over-canted and under-canted, in the back seat and the front seat. They should experiment with binding designs and binding locations. They should know that skis perform differently with step in bindings than with turn tables—especially for boots under size 7 and over 11. They should ski on D-Flex plates, and EPB's, and World Cup Spacers, and whatever technology replaces them. In short, coaches should stay curious, stay informed, and continue to learn through experience.

If coaches can transmit to their athletes some measure of curiosity about the relationship between equipment and technique, they will have given an important gift.

The second gift that coaches can give to racers is a simple love for the sport. Many coaches, under the guise of having more important work, give up skiing for fun. This is a mistake at every level of racing. Coaches should find time every day if possible, and certainly every week, to play on the mountain with the kids they coach.

Very few racers do as much free skiing as they ought to. Many coaches *tell* their athletes to do more free skiing, but they fail to lead by example. Helping young racers to become great all-mountain skiers is an important part of coaching. When free skiing, coaches can set an example of high energy, enthusiasm, and working to improve their skiing. No coach, regardless of age, should give up the quest to become a better skier. We all reach a point where it's unrealistic to think we can be faster racers. But we can still acquire new skills, and become better skiers in a variety of ways.

If you assume you have a hundred years to live, you get 1 percent older each year. Ski equipment gets 2 percent better each year. For all skiers, a net gain is possible. We should be challenged and excited by our chances to improve. Finally, we should enjoy every opportunity to free ski on a mountain with the boys and girls we coach. Racers, whether 10 or 15 or 20, pick up the attitudes and spirit of their coaches.

Coaches who help athletes develop a greater love for skiing, have given the greatest gift of all.

"If you apply the correct edge angle and pressure to a ski, and just stand on it, it will take you where you want to go."

Appreciations

More than 200 people from the alpine skiing community have made significant contributions to this book. We can't recognize all of them here; but we will long remember their friendship, their encouragement, and their wisdom. We'd like to give special thanks to the following:

Erik Ostling for contributing many days of his life to meeting our photographic needs; Thor Kallerud for sharing his knowledge, and his photos of the world's best skiers; Rob Magiera for creating our composite photographs; and Tina Vindum for her dedicated work as a model and her always cheerful spirit.

From Johnson Publishing Company—Ken Martin, Mike Reynolds, Phil Emery, Walt Borneman and Theresa Duggin for their help in producing a beautiful book.

Nan Nicklous, Wendy Hill, George Rau, Wes Pace, Christy Bertoni, Crawford Pierce, Bob Booker, and Julie Lewis for their suggestions with numerous drafts of our text.

The students and coaches of Burke Mountain Academy who have shared so much of their knowledge and enthusiasm for skiing. Finn Gundersen, George Rau and Thomas Erhard have been especially helpful.

More than a hundred people from the ski industry have provided information and support for this project. We are most grateful for the contributions of Stuart Remple, Dave Bertoni, Hans Schiessl, Roger Niele, Peter Knight, Bart Tuttle, Mel Daleboot, Bill Peterson, Jim Schaffner, Jeff Sirjane, David Larson, Steve Bagley, Rob Cartmill, Barry Woods, and Jean-Luc Diard.

John Fry and Bob LaMarche at *Snow Country* have offered valuable perspectives on many aspects of this project.

Jeff Temple and Kathy Carroll have supported this book in a variety of ways. Their interest and friendship have been important to us.

John Feig, Stephen Johnson, John Higgins, and Tim Ross have been most gracious in sharing their knowledge of physiology and sports training.

We are grateful for the hospitality extended to us by the ski schools at Alta, Snowbird, Deer Valley, Vail, Winter Park, Steamboat, and Arrowhead. Harold Harb, Sal Raio, John Gay, Mike Giesie, Alan Engen, Joe Waggoner, Mike Porter, and Wendy Hill have been especially thoughtful.

Finally, we'd like to thank Lynn Morrison for allowing us to change the "family room" in her home to a book production center; and we'd like to say *"thanks"* to Rick Stuebing and Wes Pace. They stand first among many friends whose encouragement and support have made this book possible.

Ordering Information: This book can be ordered from

THE ATHLETIC SKIER
P.O. Box 21315
Salt Lake City, Utah 84121

Enclose your name, address, and $24.95 per book plus $3.00 postage and handling. Utah residents please add state sales tax.

To order by phone, call *Reliable Racing Supply*: 1 (800) 223-4448. Master Card and Visa are accepted. Price: $24.95 plus $3.00 postage and handling. New York residents add state sales tax.

TO SCHEDULE CLINICS OR WORKSHOPS WITH THE AUTHORS, PLEASE ADDRESS CORRESPONDENCE TO THE ADDRESS ABOVE.

FOREIGN DISTRIBUTION:

CANADA **Michel Pratt Sports,** 1141 Rolland St.
Ste. Adele, P.Q., Canada G0R1L0
Phone (514) 229-7580 or (800) 265-7580.

ENGLAND **Sport N Ski,** 12-14 High Level Parade
AND Wellington Street, Gateshead
EUROPE Tyne & Wear, England. NE8 1AJ
Phone 091-478-4610   FAX 091-478-3891

AUSTRALIA **Publicity Press,** 252 Bay Street
Port Melbourne, Victoria, Australia 3207
Phone 03-646-6788

NEW ZEALAND **Meier Snow Sports Ltd.,** 16 Lake Street
Cambridge, New Zealand
Phone 0-7-827-8101   FAX 0-7-827-8999

Other books of interest:

How the Racers Ski. Autographed copies of Warren Witherell's classic work, first published in 1972, are available to readers who would like to add this historic work to their ski libraries. It can be ordered from The Athletic Skier, P.O. Box 21315, Salt Lake City, Utah 84121. Price $12.00 plus $3.00 postage and handling. Utah residents add state sales tax.

Skiing Is For Kids (and those who believe in magic). Diane Bode, whose drawings appear on pages 35, 74, 101, and 170 of *The Athletic Skier,* is the author and illustrator of this 84-page instructional coloring book. This imaginative book teaches children to ski while they color the technically accurate drawings. Lessons begin with putting on boots and end with good parallel skiing and an introduction to racing. This book is fun for children of all ages. It can be ordered from Swift Learning Resources, American Fork, Utah 84003. 1 (800) 292-2831. Price $5.95.